W
Consci

Reading this wonderful collection of stories about conscious mothers made me stop and think of my own mother and how much I miss her still, years after her death. Darlene Montgomery has compiled a treasury of personal memories that are love notes to our mothers. In this decade of the 'age wave' when millions of Baby Boomers are assisting their parents, it is a respectful memento to our mothers' lives and their planetary existence.

~ M. J. Milne, author of the New Age Sci-Fi novel,
Universal Tides: Barbed Wire Blues

"Within the words of Conscious Mothers is a silent reminder of the power that mothers have to transform us, regardless of the quality of the relationship. What we do with it speaks of our own wisdom."

~ Maxine Hyndman, Author, Speaker, Coach

"Being a parent gives us the privilege of experiencing the beauty, wonder and magic of the universe first hand. In "Conscious Mothers" we are moved and inspired to parent, from a place of wisdom, love and spiritual awareness, as it has the capacity to grow and evolve ourselves, and in turn greatly impact the world we live in."

~ Jill Hewlett, Speaker, Trainer, TV Host & Conscious Mother!

Conscious Women
Conscious Mothers

Conscious Women
Conscious Mothers

*True Stories of Wisdom and Awareness
on the Path of Motherhood*

Darlene Montgomery

From the Social Issues Series:
White Knight's Remarkable Women

White Knight Books
Toronto, Canada

Published in 2007 by
White Knight Books, a division of Bill Belfontaine Ltd.
Suite 103, One Benvenuto Place, Toronto Ontario Canada M4V 2L1
T. 416-925-6458 F. 416-925-4165 • e-mail whitekn@istar.ca
www.whiteknightbooks.ca

White Knight Books gratefully acknowledges the financial support of the Ontario Media Development Corporation and the Ontario Arts Council.

Ordering information

CANADA	UNITED STATES
White Knight Book Distribution Services Ltd.	APG Distributors
c/o Georgetown Terminal Warehouses	(Associated Publishers' Group)
34 Armstrong Avenue,	1501 County Hospital Road
Georgetown ON, L7G 4R9	Nashville, TN, 37218 USA
T: 1-866-485-5556 F: 1-866-485-6665	T: 1-888-725-2606 F: 1-800-510-3650

First printing: February 2007

Library and Archives Canada Cataloguing in Publication

Conscious women, conscious mothers : true stories of wisdom and
awareness on the path of motherhood / Darlene Montgomery.
Includes bibliographical references.
ISBN 978-0-9780570-8-4
1. Motherhood. I. Montgomery, Darlene, 1958-
HQ759.M66 2007   306.874'3   C2007-901013-X

Cover and Text Design: Karen Thomas Petherick
Editing: Judy Prang
Back Cover Picture: Christine Switzer
Cover photo: ©Shutterstock
Printed and Bound in Canada

Dedication

To All Mothers Everywhere

Contents

4. Healing to Move Ahead

5. The Miracle of Birth

6. Life's Most Interesting Moments

Acknowledgements

Conscious Mothers has been a joy to compile. With each new story that came across my desk, I was more astounded by the spiritual insight and depth of experience from each writer. I am so grateful to be part of the process of creating these books, but the greatest reward came through interacting with the many women contributors. Thanks to each and every one of you who shared your story, your challenges and your breakthroughs.

I often hear from readers who have gained so much spiritually, emotionally and mentally from that hidden ingredient inside the stories in the Conscious Women books. I know that many of you faced deep fears to write your stories and for that I thank you. It is only because of your willingness to delve deeper that the stories offer a medicine for the Soul.

Thanks to my many good and true friends on the path of ECK-ANKAR, Jane and Paul Pulkys, Lily Bedikian, Yolande Savoie, Jerry and Jo Leonard, Janet Matthews, Laura Reave, Stan Burgess, Thomas Drayton, Barbara Russo-Smith, Marlene Chapelle, Barbara Allport, Marilyn Milne, Eva Lemster, Eitan Hassan and Carol Lidstone who have shared those special moments of insight and clarity on the path. I thank you with all my heart. A special thanks to Karen Petherick Thomas for her cover designs and to Bill Belfontaine for his daring and determination to bring inspiring books to the world.

Thank you to my Mother, Mary. You have always stood by me through all the trials and have helped me in so many ways to be the woman I am today.

Thanks to my wonderful daughter who has stood by me through years of self-discovery, risk-taking and self-exploration. You're my best friend.

Thank you to each and every one who participated in creating this book.

And finally, a special thanks, to Sri Harold Klemp for both outer and inner support.

~ *Darlene Montgomery*

Introduction

Writing a book about Motherhood is perhaps the most natural of all the books I've done.

Being the mother of a wonderful daughter, I've watched a part of myself unfold in a way which is only possible through first growing a child inside you, then giving birth, nurturing another soul through the many stages of life: from infancy where a child is all trusting and wise, through the school years where their identity is shaped, to teenage-hood when the individuality is tested and tried, and into adulthood where our child is still learning the lessons of his or her destiny.

I've seen myself in my daughter: the learning, the growth, and the beauty. I've learned to step back and let her grow. I've learned to trust God more and to know that there is continuity to life.

A mother's love is so close to God's love in that it is a selfless love, so unconditional and yet strong enough to contain life. From that love is born a kind of freedom, for we always know that with motherhood comes the time when our child must fly.

Motherhood is a universal yet individual experience, whether it is through adoption, fostering, the joy of our first born, the first tooth, the first day of school, graduation and the many stages and steps along the way. You've shared your milestones, your losses, your healings and your heartaches. Thanks to all of you who shared from the heart so that we could take another step on our path of mother-hood. These stories are a testimony to the everyday miracles in our lives.

~ *Darlene Montgomery*

1

On Mothers and Daughters

A mother is the truest friend we have, when trials, heavy
and sudden, fall upon us; when adversity takes the place
of prosperity; when friends who rejoice with us in our
sunshine, desert us; when troubles thicken around us,
still will she cling to us, and endeavor by her kind pre-
cepts and counsels to dissipate the clouds of darkness,
and cause peace to return to our hearts.

~ Washington Irving

My Mother – A Mystery

The best and most beautiful things
in the world cannot be seen
or even touched.
They must be felt with the heart.
~ Helen Keller

"Can I keep the minnow, Mom?" I pleaded, as the tiny creature swam frantically around the confines of my Dixie cup. "I'll take very good care of it."

"If you mean what you say, Sheila, then you'll wade into the river and set it free." It would take me years to understand what my mother meant that day. As a child, I felt I could own my prizes, even my mother, who was my best treasure. But I was wrong.

That summer, she created magic and adventure every day when she took us to the beach, down to the noisy St. Lawrence River. Following a flurry of tasks, orchestrated by my thirty-six-year-old mother, we left the farmhouse my father had rented for the summer.

Our small caravan donned white caps and stood on the grass waiting for her to take the lead. She carried Frank. Behind her Kay, carting soft drinks and diapers, took Michael's hand. Maureen toted pails, shovels, Dixie cups and a can opener, lastly I clutched sandwiches and the red Scotch blanket.

Once across the road, we marched in single file along the shoulder. Often my mother's head turned towards us to assure herself that we were following closely behind. We took a right turn one thousand feet along the highway, down a path blasted into existence and obscured by foliage. Negotiating in the loose shade of the deep descent, we grabbed tree branches to keep from falling. Before we could count to fifty, the path ended, and a panorama of wind, sand, rock and water lay at our feet.

We walked on cool, rippled sand between massive rocks until my mother found a place somewhat protected from the wind. She spread the blanket on the sand, anchoring the corners with stones. Then we ran to the river's edge to find water trapped between rocks deep enough to chill the soft drinks and then we'd scour the shoreline for seaweed to pop between our fingers. My mother stayed anchored like a stone to the blanket. She bounced Frank on her knees and collected coarse sand for Michael. We sisters leapt from one rock to another, daring each other with more difficult jumps. Our pigtails flew behind us. My mother worked frantically to create a castle that would keep my little brother Michael from the lure of the rocks. She sat there with her sons, each battling for an arm. At lunch we all ran back to the safety of the blanket. There we chose numbers to win the half bottle of red cream soda, with the losers reduced to drinking their soda from Dixie cups.

My mother never ate lunch with us, but drawing in her knees and cupping her chin, she'd listen to our adventures. When we finished eating, she'd tell Kay to sit at one end of the blanket, me at the other, placing the little ones between us. 'Watch over each other; I won't be long.' Off came the pink and white-striped halter and the sun skirt, and with them the trappings of motherhood.

In their stead stood a tall, handsome, big-boned woman in a

black bathing suit. Without looking back at us, without pausing to test the frigid water, she'd wade in past her waist, sprinkle both shoulders with icy water and in seconds dive, disappearing into the St. Lawrence. We held onto one another on the blanket, afraid we had lost her, afraid she had left us, afraid the river had claimed her. In those long seconds I felt lonely, and small.

Then, with the grace of a dolphin she'd rise from the river with water tumbling from her dark curls and begin her swim. The smooth cutting stroke and confident rhythm of her long arms propelled this amazon into a thing of beauty that years before had captured my father's heart and now took ours. In these rarefied moments she was someone quite apart from us, and we burst with tenderness that this remarkable wet creature belonged to us. Then, perhaps for the joyous freedom she found in the river, my mother would laugh aloud, becoming once more the 'laughing Margaret' of her university days. From afar, leaning forward on the blanket, we'd sit in awe.

Yet, she always came back to us. In she'd walk, luminous, aglitter with diamond drops falling from her shoulders.

"The water was grand today," she'd say.

And that was the end of her freedom. As she sat on the blanket, the sun and wind conspired to erase the watery signs of her brief escape. What I couldn't see then was that my mother had returned to her source, just like the minnow, for the short time she left us. Once she was dressed, from the pocket of her pink skirt, she'd take three water-color paint brushes and give them to her girls; then she reached for her sandwich. We'd run to fill the Dixie cups with water, select a rock, and begin to paint water sketches that too soon evaporated. Shortly, my mother, with Frank in her arms, would lead us back up the hill.

Today, standing alone on a sandstone cliff above the St.

Lawrence, whipped by steady blasts of wind rising from the mighty flow of the river, I search for my mother across the whitecaps. There was a reason for the fear I harbored of losing her when I was five. What I'd dreaded most had simply crouched, waiting behind the years, waiting for time to claim her. Yet as I turn slowly from the river and begin to climb back down the hill, I hear my mother's laughter in the gusting winds.

~ *Sheila Kindellan-Sheehan*

Acts of Kindness

Small acts of kindness allow me to touch souls with
another person – to reach out over the great divide
 and brush for a moment the hand and heart of another.

An act of kindness is never wasted. It benefits the
giver as much or more than the receiver. Anyone who
gives with the heart strengthens the muscle within
themselves; it is the aerobic training of the spirit.

I will not expect soul to just enter my life by
chance. I will prepare myself, clean the vehicle that
is me, resolve conflicts that tie my mind up and drain
my energy. When I am less self-centered, I am able to
take the personhood of another into consideration.

I enjoy being kind for kindness' sake.
"And this more human love (which will consummate
itself infinitely, thoughtfully and gently, and well
and clearly in binding and loosing) will be something
like that which we are preparing with struggle and
toil, the love which consists in the mutual guarding,
bordering and saluting of two solitudes."

~ Rainer Maria Rilke

It's a Piece of Cake

Keep your face to the sunshine
and you cannot see the shadow.
~ Helen Keller

With a huge sigh of relief, I learned she would be okay. Through a series of small miracles, the endometrial cancer had been discovered early, and dealt with quickly. Her recovery was slow, but complete, and I was so grateful to God for returning her to us. I was absolutely terrified of losing my mother. We always expected her to live to be a very old lady, but she was only sixty-nine.

Then, one night after my contemplation, an inner voice said to me, clearly, and briefly: "You have five years left with your mother."

Completely astounded, I told no one. I hoped I was wrong – maybe it was fear coming from my subconscious.

Still, I changed my relationship with her. With those words never far away, I began to cherish every moment we had. I encouraged her to take more vitamins and supplements. I changed our family dynamic and began to wrap my arms around her every time I saw her. When she called and began to rattle on, even if I were busy I would swallow my impatience, and chat – grateful that it was her voice, knowing one day it would not be there.

When the five years came and went, I decided I must have been wrong. A year later, I had put it out of my mind altogether. Then in January 1998, exactly six years later, she was diagnosed with Acute Leukemia. She was incredibly ill, and in that moment, I knew. For some reason we'd had a reprieve, but the time was up. Totally devastated, I fell apart again. My terror of losing her was more than I could bear. I felt like a five-year-old child as I sobbed out of control.

Once her treatments began at Toronto's Princess Margaret Hospital, I began to tell her I loved her each time I left her. Uncomfortable with this simple expression of emotion, she could only pat my hand and say, "Me too."

One day I sat at home and did a focused, visualization exercise. While I sang HU, an ancient and powerful love song to God, I invited all the spiritual guides I knew to surround her hospital bed. I visualized the light from their beings filling the room, and surrounding her. Then, I turned the results over to spirit, and simply sent her all the love I had in my heart. Because of my precognition of this event, I felt it must be all part of some divine plan, and I was reluctant to interfere with it. Although it was difficult, I did not to ask them to heal her, or try and heal her myself. Somehow I managed to surrender it all to spirit.

By June it appeared the full remission we sought had been achieved. My sister arrived from British Columbia with her two boys, and we had a time of love and joy as a family. We had barbeques, took a lot of pictures, and went out to dinner and the theatre. We told a lot of jokes, laughed a lot, and had a lot of hugs.

Then, in July we learned that remission had not been achieved after all. When I realized she had only three or four months left, I was overcome with grief. When she left I wanted no regrets, nothing outstanding or left unsaid, so I decided to give her my all. But giving to my mother was difficult. Her lack of self-love meant she had a hard time accepting love; low self worth had been her lifetime companion. I sat by her bed a lot, and silently sang the HU. I became committed to helping her learn to accept my love. Perhaps it would allow her to take a bigger step when she finally did leave her body.

My sister returned in late summer, and the next day our mother, who had been home for a short while re-entered hospital. Together, we began to look for ways of giving to her what she could accept. We helped her brush her teeth, and use the bathroom. We brought her special books, and as she became weaker, we read to her. Often, we sang to her. When Ruth had to return home to her family, I carried on, doing many of the things she had done for me when I was a child. Often she said, "You need to leave now, you've done enough, I don't want you to bother with that," and the like. But every day before I left, I would put my arms around her and say, "I love you."

She began to get used to this, responding at first hesitantly and then more easily. She began to receive it, and accept it. One day she finally said, "Yes, I love you too."

Her eyes became sparkly, and when she smiled, she looked like she was lit from within. I was grateful she was not in pain, and did not require the numbing effects of narcotics. With her appetite gone, eating was a challenge, so every night I would arrive to help her eat dinner. The hospital food was abysmal, and it broke my heart to see her disappointment when confronted with it. Each day she ate less, but would not allow me to bring her anything.

Canadian Thanksgiving arrived. For many years it had been just Mum, Dad and me. I was determined we would share it one more time. Between hospital visits, I made a turkey dinner in stages. On Sunday I packed a bag with good china and silver, linen, and plastic wineglasses. I carved the bird, slicing her favorite dark meat, really thin. Then along with two TV tables, I packed and trundled it all down to the hospital on a luggage cart.

Dad was already there, and I said: "Okay you guys, I need your help. Just let me do this okay? I need you to just sit there, not fuss, and ALLOW me to do this. Okay?" Laughingly, they agreed.

I heated the food in the kitchen next door, and served the meal, giving Mum the finely sliced turkey and homemade mashed potatoes and gravy made with love. I asked my father to say the Grace, as he has always done. And then he and I watched as Mum ate every bit of food on that plate. All the work had been worthwhile, and with a lump in my throat I experienced a bittersweet kind of happiness.

Mid-week I called my sister and told her it was time. She arrived on Friday. On Sunday I accompanied my father to church, at his request. Ruth went early to the hospital, and arrived in time to be with Mum when she died that morning. Each of us was exactly where we were supposed to be.

We all have our own relationship with Divine Spirit. For some it's very overt, with a lot of inner sight, light and sound, and intimate contact with inner masters and spiritual guides. Others of us have a relationship based more on knowing, and a feeling. We are aware of how our outer life reflects the inner truths. Most of the time, I fall into this latter category.

However, I have several gifted friends in the first category. One, my dear friend Alex was at the funeral, and although I looked up hopefully into the great ceiling arches, Alex was the one who saw her. Her description of Mum appearing in a radiant peachy coral color, with a joyful smile on her face brought us a great deal of peace.

The following week I called another close, dear friend in Florida. Frannie is a 'Spiritual Intuitive' and although she works with a different line of Masters than me, she is often aware of the presence of my spiritual guide when we speak. She invited me to call her at 10:15

Friday, and before we began she would invite my mother to join us. I was a little startled, but could only agree. My Mum knew of Frannie, and that she did this kind of work.

The time finally arrived, and when I called, the first thing Frannie said was, "Janet, your mother is already here. She came early to visit, and just made herself right at home. She's sitting on my bed, and we have been getting to know each other." When Frannie described her as wearing a radiant peachy coral colored dress, I had to tell myself to keep breathing.

"She has a little dog on her lap," reported Frannie. I quickly realized it was her beloved fox terrier Laddie, from her childhood. Apparently Laddie had been waiting for her for all these years, and when she left her body, was right there to greet her with love and joy! She told Frannie she didn't go anywhere without him.

"Janet," Frannie said, "all your masters are here. There are hundreds of them – lining up and out the doors. My house is just crackling; the energy in here is incredible! They are here with your mother, and she is being held in the higher vibration of the energy field of the masters. She couldn't be in this energy field by herself."

I had learned I would have the love and presence of the masters to escort me across the borders of death when my time came, and so would everyone that I love. The connection of the heart would allow this wonderful gift. I had always hoped it was true, but I now *know* from this experience that it *is* true!

"I'll receive information from your mother in something like balls of thought energy," said Frannie, "then I'll translate, or relay it to you. Even though your mum is still weak and recovering from her ordeal, she is very excited about your visit. She has so much to share with you."

Through Frannie, my mother then told me how much she loved

me, and how wonderful it was to have no pain, and nothing restricting her from speaking the truth from her heart. She told me how much she appreciated me, and that I stayed true to myself. She wanted me to know that during the course of her illness, as she watched me, she saw a lot of parts of herself that she did not love. The whole last five months of her life was about seeing, for the first time in her life, her true self in my eyes. In the end, that's what helped her to leave, in the pure love that came from my eyes. She had received it.

She told me in the moment she went to the light, she understood it all; in that moment everything in her life flashed before her, and she saw it like a tapestry. She instantly understood everything she'd ever heard from me, or anyone else, about spirit or truth, that she was supposed to get, but didn't, when she was here in her body. She told me she now understood why I'd get so frustrated with her, because in the body, she didn't understand it and couldn't comprehend it, because she had so much fear. She told me she stayed longer than necessary in her body for her own growth, and that during the last five months in particular, she had to do a "discovering." This involved working with some memories so she could let go of them, so these memories wouldn't hold her to the earth too long after she'd left.

She told me I needed to tell people the reason for a long illness is because the mind is not allowing the memories of the past to surface and be understood. The greater the mind's resistance to facing these issues, the longer the illness will be. She said that was why I was with her, because during her illness, my energy lifted her, and I could "hold a space" and bring the energy in to help her do this work.

She told me her leaving at this point in my life would allow me to now go and be in my life's purpose – to do what I came here to do. She told me this was all part of a divine plan we made together, before this life began. She told me that if I just remembered my own self worth, the next three months would be "a piece of cake."

She told me when she arrived on the other side, Laddie was waiting for her, along with all the members of her family that had gone before her. She was not spending too much time with them, choosing instead to go to the temple in the inner world where she is, to heal and learn. Apparently when one has had a long illness before crossing over, there is a period of time required in the inner worlds for healing, and soul goes to a kind of rest home to recover.

She told me Laddie goes nowhere without her, and she's spending her time doing higher work now. When she chooses to incarnate again, she will come back knowing the Masters' truth.

Our visit continued for over an hour, and before she left, she said how much she loved me, and she thanked me again for all the love I had given her.

Frannie then said, "She's kissing you now. It's so strange I can see her here in my room, but I can also see her there with you – there really is no separation." And then she faded, and gently and quietly left, accompanied by the masters.

This experience changed my life in a way so profound I don't even have words to describe it. The truth of everything I'd ever studied and read was validated that day. I know where my mother is, who she's with, and what she's doing. My own process of grieving had mostly been completed during her illness, and I was stunned to discover that after this experience, my healing from her loss was almost total. The love and peace which entered my heart that day stayed with me, and remains with me still.

I have three images of her; one from her life – healthy and busy being a wife and mother; one from the nine months of her illness, struggling to be in her body; and one from the present – radiant in her peachy coral, reunited with her beloved Laddie, recovering and full of love in the company of the masters. It is more than I could have ever hoped. When I miss her, I think of where she is, and her final words of wisdom to me: "Just remember your own self worth, and it will be a piece of cake."

~ *Janet Matthews*

A Love Everlasting

Mom and I were made from the same mold, the same straight brown hair, the same nearsighted brown eyes and physique. Mom was my mainstay. Despite all my scholastic achievements and student activities, I was shy and insecure, and she was always there for me. Mom taught social studies at my high school, so all my friends knew her and loved her too.

I was 15 when Mom was diagnosed with lupus and hospitalized for five months. She recovered and went back to teaching, and everything seemed normal. A year later she caught a simple cold that grew into a serious case of pneumonia. Within a week, she was gone. My world abruptly shattered. The door slammed shut on so many possibilities. All the questions I had had about Mom's life and feelings, about my own blossoming womanhood, about seemingly trivial things – like the recipes for our favorite Christmas cookies and Mom's famous lemon meringue pie – now none of those questions would be answered. Mom would never be there, and I was left feeling deeply sad and alone.

My whole personality seemed to change at that point. The open and idealistic person I'd been was replaced with bitterness and sarcasm. It was as if my heart was armored with grief and guilt. I was haunted by images of my mother's unhappiness. I remembered her sitting on the edge of her bed, weeping, while the rest of the family argued. I remembered so many times when it seemed I could have done more to comfort her.

In my sophomore year of college, I learned to meditate and slowly began to emerge from the numbing shell of protection that I had built around myself. Meditation opened the door to dealing with my grief effectively. I'd sit with my eyes closed, and healing tears would flow.

One morning while I was meditating, I remembered caring for Mom when she had returned from the hospital. I had resented the fact that I had to dress her bedsores when I really wanted to hang out with my friends. A flood of guilt and shame welled up in me as I recalled how selfish I'd been.

Just then a thought burst into my head. It was a story Mom had told me about my grandfather, who was stricken with throat cancer when she was eight years old. Before he died, he said to her, "Evelyn, remember this; if anything happens to me and you really need me, call and I will be there for you."

Mom told me that when she was in college, she fell in love with a young man who broke her heart. She felt so distraught that she called out to her father inside herself. She said, "Suddenly, I felt him standing in my dorm room. I felt so loved by him that I knew everything would be all right."

It seemed worth a try, so I cried out to Mom in my mind. "I'm sorry," I sobbed, over and over again. A change came over the room as time stood still. And then I felt a cloak of peace spread over me. I heard my mother say, "All is understood. All is forgiven. There is no need for regrets." At that moment all the burden of guilt I had carried around was released and replaced with a sense of freedom like I'd never felt before.

A few years later on the eve of my wedding to a wonderful man named Tony, I found myself missing Mom more than I had in years. I longed for her to share the celebration: I needed her blessing and warmth. Once again I called out to Mom to ask for her presence to be with me on my special day.

The day of the wedding was sunny and glorious – I was soon caught up in the festivities. Afterward, my long-time friend Marilyn approached with a tear-streaked face. She said she wasn't sad; she just needed to talk to me. We made our way to a private corner of the hall.

"Do you know anyone named Forshay?" she asked.

"Well yes," I answered. "My mother's maiden name was Forshar, but it was changed from the French 'Forshay'. Why do you ask?"

Marilyn spoke more quietly then. "During your wedding ceremony, an incredible thing happened. I saw you and Tony surrounded by a light and a presence that was filled with love for you. It was so beautiful it made me cry. And I kept getting that the name Forshay was associated with it."

I was too stunned to say anything. Marilyn continued, "And there was a message that came for you with it. The presence wanted you to know that you will always be loved, to never doubt that, and that this love will always come to you through your friends."

By this time, I was crying as Marilyn and I held each other. I finally understood that death could not break a connection forged in love, and that my mother had always been there in spirit all these years. To this day, I will sometimes catch a glimpse of something in the eyes of a friend or loved one, or even in my own eyes in the mirror, and I know my mother is still here, loving me.

~ *Suzanne Thomas Lawlor*

Mother and Daughter Reunion

Nothing is predestined: The obstacles of your past can
become the gateways that lead to new beginnings.
~ Ralph Blum

It was Veterans' Day and I was in labor with my second child. Knowing it would be too late by the time my husband got home from work, I asked my neighbor Mary to drive me to the hospital. Focused on the destination, neither of us noticed the crowd-lined sidewalks and that marching toward our car was an array of people clad in different military uniforms, all waving American flags.

Mary panicked and stopped the car in the middle of the road when a motorcycle police officer yelled, "Hey lady are you blind? You're in the middle of a parade!" He approached the car and pounded furiously on the window. Speechless, Mary just pointed at my bulging stomach.

The officer's demeanor changed instantly. He held up his hand motioning the procession to slow down and gestured for the parade to spread out. It was a remarkable sight. The marchers never skipped a beat as they divided into two lines, making space big enough for our car to get through. I felt like a celebrity having a police escort to the hospital.

"This baby is going to be something special," I thought. Little did I know how special. I delivered Baby Elaine thirty minutes later with very little pain. A different kind of pain was yet to come. I didn't understand the many symbols that were alerting me and the impact her birth would have on my life.

Early on a strong confident character trait emerged in Elaine. One evening I was in the kitchen preparing lunch when I heard Ed, Elaine's older brother holler "OUCH". I looked up to see Elaine, toy truck in hand, bending over to kiss Ed's cheek. She'd used it to hit him on the head when he wouldn't comply with her demands to play.

In the coming years I was increasingly unnerved by her behavior. No matter how many times I reminded her not to eat or drink anything unless it was given to her by someone from our family, she always ignored me. This resulted in numerous visits to the hospital emergency room to have her stomach pumped. I especially remember the time she and her friend had a tea party in the backyard and ate a poison mushroom they found growing there.

As a child Elaine had beautiful shoulder length strawberry blonde hair. She looked adorable when I curled it for special occasions. For everyday I kept it braided, even though she hated all the tugging and pulling. She constantly pleaded with me for a short haircut. I always said no.

One afternoon, I was mending some clothes while watching television and Elaine sat beside me reading a book. As I rose to answer the phone, I noticed Elaine going upstairs to the bathroom. Soon after, she reappeared holding out both her hands. In one was the scissors, in the other, a beautiful strawberry blonde braid. Of course I cried.

Two months after starting kindergarten I got a phone call from her teacher, "How is Elaine feeling?" she asked. Elaine had not been in school for three days and the teacher was calling to inquire about her health. It seemed I had a six-year-old truant.

I finally sought professional help by taking Elaine to a child psychologist. "Just try giving her more of your attention. She'll be fine." was his diagnosis. I wondered where he got his license to practice. I had no other recourse but to grin and bear it, hoping she would outgrow what I thought were her attempts to drive me crazy.

Her teen years brought new problems and a new approach. By then I was exploring alternative means to understand my life and my relationship with my daughter. I decided I'd go for a past life reading to learn more about the factors which were influencing our relationship. The reading revealed that Elaine and I had had many incarnations together, always in a family relationship. In each lifetime I had caused her much grief with my manipulative ways. It seemed I was a controller. I also learned that Elaine and I had made a different soul contract this lifetime. We had decided to change those conditions.

Her mission was to speak up for what she believed, and be in control of her life. Mine was to let go of control and accept Elaine as she was. Knowing the reason for our choosing to be together helped, but we would also be influenced by the temptation to fall into old patterns. It wouldn't be easy to break them, as the next years showed us.

Her resentment of me festered. My unhappiness with her grew.

Elaine got her driver's license at sixteen. The first time she headed out on her own, she made a turn too sharply and hit a parked car. It was one of many incidents that kept driving us apart, no pun intended. I just wasn't getting the lesson.

It was when I found the teachings of Eckankar, a religion which showed me how to interpret dreams, both waking and sleeping, that things started to change. With a new awareness of how unusual events in our life can be looked at as waking dreams, I reflected back on the day she was born and the parade that foretold what our life together would be like.

The dream told me that her arrival on Veterans' day with a parade and police escort was not by chance. I saw that each branch of the armed forces was symbolic of our many different lifetimes of battle; the American flags represented the search for freedom. The hospital was the battlefield were I was about to meet my adversary, a veteran Soul coming back to do combat with me, wearing her spiritual armor to fight for her right to express herself with the confidence she had lacked in her past lives. The name of the hospital was Braddock General. I found out that *General Braddock* was commander of the British Forces in North America and was responsible for building a road to expand the western frontier. Braddock's Road was the first road open to the public for travel through southwestern Pennsylvania, where I lived.

The parting of the parade, a parting that led to Braddock General Hospital, foretold that there would be a new road paved for me and my daughter. This road could, this time around, finally change the outcome of our life together.

With this new understanding, I asked for guidance on how to begin to mend our relationship. During my dreams I received answers, especially about our past life relationships. Some were very upsetting.

Many of the dreams showed how I never took time to listen to what Elaine was telling me and never respected her right to free choice. My contract for this life had been to learn to grant this soul, my daughter, freedom while recognizing her strengths.

Then one day, after Elaine was a married woman with children of her own, I summoned up the courage to face her. I was ready for our relationship to be healed and was hoping she was too.

I knew I'd be seeing her at the hospital. My Mom was nearing death and Elaine, who worked full time in a nursing home, was selflessly stopping by each day to help with her grandmother's care.

In the doorway of the room I stopped, fascinated by Elaine as she tended my mother with the utmost love. I stood and watched her angelic moves and thought, "I wish my daughter loved me that much." In a flash I felt a light slap on the face from an invisible hand. The kind of smack someone gives to awaken you from unconsciousness.

I backed away and went outside to think. Could it be the hand of God teaching me about unconditional love? Was He waking me up to the fact I was running out of chances to get it right this lifetime?

That day Elaine and I did talk. At first we played verbal ping-pong, throwing blame back and forth at each other. Then I remembered the tingle of that invisible hand slapping me and my heart began to open wide with love. Elaine must have felt the change in me, because soon we both had tears running down our faces. We forgave each other and reached an agreement that we would treat each other with more love and freedom. Our conversation that day ended with a big hug. It was a real mother and daughter reunion.

Today we have a wonderful relationship full of grace and warmth. Elaine is my daughter, my teacher, my friend. The healing is complete; the old pattern broken. I love her unconditionally.

~ *Betty Jane Rapin*

Coming Home to Oz

One night many years ago, when I was expecting my second child, I had a dream, which, in retrospect, can only be called prophetic. I opened my eyes to see an old man sitting at the end of my bed. He had an air of wisdom about him and wanted to talk about the child I would soon give birth to. He asked whether I wanted a boy or a girl, but when I said that I already had a daughter and would therefore like a boy, he replied, "Well, I am sending you a girl, a very troubled girl who needs a strong family. She will need your guidance." He went on to explain that my child was an old soul who had been very badly abused in a past life and that she was coming to me to learn to trust herself and other people. This experience continued for some time and when I awoke in the morning I remarked to myself on what a strange dream it had been. It had seemed so real.

My second daughter, Eve, was born on a lovely summer's day, on July 8th, 1984. In spite of the dream, she was extremely easy to care for. She slept through the night by six weeks of age and hardly ever cried. Born at 8 pounds, 10 ounces, she continued to grow into a pleasant, cherubic baby, with the appetite of a horse. Our friends found it amusing to see how much our little baby could consume. I didn't know then how ironic that detail would turn out to be.

As Eve grew older, there was a beautiful ethereal quality about her, as though she was in this world and yet not fully of it. She developed into a gifted artist, was very intelligent and excelled in mathematics, eventually placing third in a provincial mathematics competition. Amidst all of these blessings, the warning of my dream was forgotten, until Eve's fourteenth year.

That year was an incredibly difficult one for our family. My husband suffered a very serious break to his leg and was unable to work for seven months. Because we had depended solely on his income, I found myself suddenly scrambling to get work in order to sustain our family of five.

That same year, both of my parents were admitted to separate hospitals: my father for heart problems and my mother for a hip replacement which developed complications. My energy was so consumed with running from one hospital to the other, and dealing with the financial strain and daily stress at home, that at first I did not notice the changes in Eve, who had slowly and subtly gone from her happy chatty self, to a withdrawn and silent child. But when her eating habits changed dramatically, she became obsessive about fat content, and began exercising constantly, I became concerned. I took her to our family doctor, but he dismissed my worries and told me I was just being silly. 'Maybe he's right,' I thought. 'Perhaps I'm just overreacting.' But in my heart I knew that something was wrong.

Time passed and Eve continued to lose weight. Even my friends were beginning to notice, and I would sometimes find her exercising in her bedroom in the middle of the night. But again, when I took her to a specialist on eating disorders, I was told that Eve was a lovely slim girl and not to worry. Reassured, I again turned my attention back to my parents, whose health went into further decline. I was virtually living at two hospitals, with little time to pay attention to the situation at home. It was winter then and it seemed that Eve was at home as rarely as I was.

When warmer weather finally arrived, our family decided to spend the first holiday weekend at our cottage, which was a three hour drive from the city. It had been a long hard winter and we were looking forward to this time away. The weather was fabulous and it felt great to be free of winter's bundled layers.

I was outside enjoying the sun when Eve appeared on the dock in her bathing suit. As I glanced up and saw her, my heart constricted. 'Oh my God!' I thought, 'How could I have been so blind?' She looked like a skeleton, her bones protruding through her skin, and her feet were noticeably purple from lack of circulation. I discovered later that Eve, who was 5-foot 4-inches tall, weighed only 82 pounds!

Shocked and alarmed, my husband and I packed the children right back into the car and headed straight for Toronto's Sick Kids Hospital, the only hospital in our area known to have a program for eating disorders. As Eve was admitted to the Eating Disorder Ward, a mixture of relief, fear, guilt, and anger swept through me, followed by a horrible sadness. How could I have been such a bad parent? I berated myself. I was extremely grateful to think that Eve was now getting the help she needed, but how had I failed to notice that my daughter was starving herself to death? After admitting her, I sat in my car in the hospital parking lot and sobbed for hours. This was to mark the beginning of an intensely dark time in my life.

The next day my family was interviewed by a team of physiatrists, three of them behind one-way mirrors. They watched to see how we interacted and what our family dynamics were. I was willing to do anything to help my child get well, but having to submit to this type of scrutiny, on top of everything we were already going through, was unbearable, not to mention how difficult it was on my other two children. Finally, we were informed that Eve would not be released until her weight had reached one hundred pounds. I felt like I was falling apart.

Slowly, over time, Eve's weight started to climb, but I began to realize that she was still not getting well, mentally or emotionally. The hospital ward was an unhealthy place, more like a jail where the inmates were force-fed and the kids taught each other brilliant tricks to avoid eating. However, during her stay, I did learn a lot about Eve's disease. Most importantly, I learned that Anorexia isn't really about food, but about control and self worth.

I waited for Eve to reach her target weight so that I could regain control over my child's healing. Finally, after eight weeks, Eve's weight hit one hundred pounds and she was released from the hospital. This was a monumental achievement, however other parents at the hospital warned me that the real roller coaster ride was now about to begin.

The hospital therapist had warned me that Eve was depressed and recommended that she go on anti-depressants, but I resisted the advice, feeling that it would only mask the real problem. After she was released, I found an excellent therapist for her and was confident that we would finally get to the bottom of the problem. And Eve's weight did eventually become acceptable, yet she remained incredibly distant. Sometimes I would find her in tears, still so sad. I loved her so much, but was at a loss as to how I could help this precious soul to gain the trust and self-worth she would need to get fully well.

During this entire ordeal, I prayed daily for guidance and strength. More than anything, I wanted my child to be well. I wanted her to know her own worth and to experience joy in her life once again. At one point during this period, my youngest daughter, Emma, drew me a picture of a heart filled with four circles: one labeled "Hope," another "Courage," the other, "Pride," and the last, "Strength." This act of love from my ten year old lifted my spirits immensely and gave me the courage to continue battling the demon that had been ripping our lives apart. I still have the picture hanging framed in my room.

That summer Eve was booked as crew on a ship for two weeks. I felt hopeful that this could be a turning point for her, but then, the day before she was to leave, I found marks on her arms showing that she'd been cutting herself. I became hysterical and refused to let her go on the trip because I was terrified she would throw herself overboard in the dark of night. She pleaded with me to let her go and, after speaking to her therapist, who felt that the sun and exercise would be good for Eve, I hesitantly agreed.

When Eve returned from her holiday I knew we had to try something different. It was time to admit that she needed anti-depressants. We found a new doctor who could prescribe the medication Eve needed, and once she began taking the anti-depressants she did start to improve a bit, attending school more regularly and getting more involved with life – but she still wasn't happy. At this point I had tried everything I could, but she remained distant, hardly talked, and came and went like a shadow. I knew that I was still treating her like a sick child and that I needed to learn to trust her again if I was ever to help her trust herself, but I didn't know how to do it.

Meanwhile, life went on for the rest of us. My youngest daughter, Emma, had been taking riding lessons and I regularly drove her to the riding stables. I began to spend a lot of time around the barns and it was there that I remembered my long-forgotten love for horses, which had begun over thirty years before, when my father owned a farm. It was while I was hanging around the barn, waiting for Emma that I heard about a horseback riding program for beginners. Suddenly, I got the idea to sign Eve and me up for lessons. I would share my own love of horses with her!

The first few times Eve and I drove to the stable, the air between us was very strained. I tried desperately to have a conversation with my daughter, but received only single word responses, and eventually resorted to the radio. Soon, however, we were riding regularly and I began to notice a change in Eve. For the first time in many years she was excited about something. And then, after a few sessions, a funny thing started to happen. Eve fell in love with riding, becoming as passionate about it as her sister Emma and I were. Our car rides were now spent chatting excitedly about horses and riding. What's more, Eve started to laugh again! It's amazing what a miracle a smile can be. For us, it was tangible proof that the deeper healing process was finally underway.

Eventually, we made the decision to buy our own horse. I figured that the cost was about the same as the therapy, and we got far more back in return. This horse, which we named the Wizard of Oz, is one of the most magical things to have happened in Eve's life. Riding Oz has given her a great sense of empowerment and love in her life, which has led to an incredible transformation. He is a source of love for her and, just as importantly, provides an opportunity for her to give unconditional love to another being. On the days that she rides him, she gets to the barn extra early and spends over an hour brushing his coat, and when they are finished riding she always takes him to the best patches of grass to graze. It doesn't matter if it is pouring rain; she makes sure that he gets this special time.

Eve has been riding for two years now and is a changed person. Through her time with Oz, she has learned, not only to control her own emotional responses in order to be a better rider, but to trust and give the reigns over to her horse when necessary, just as we must surrender to life once we have done all that we must do. And in finding her rhythm with Oz, she regained the rhyme and rhythm of her own life. She has graduated from college, is living on her own, and is a young woman full of joy, passion, and purpose. It was a long, difficult journey, but the real inner healing began with love – Eve's love of riding and her love for a horse – which helped show her the way home to herself.

~ *Christine Switzer*

My Mother, My Spiritual Teacher

They say in Buddhism that there are two people whose gifts are so great, try as you may you could never repay them. The first person is your mother for giving you life and the second is the person who introduced you to the dharma, or spiritual teachings. My mother gave me both gifts. We tend to take our mothers for granted and think that what they offer us is just what all moms give. As I get older I see my mother more as an individual and am amazed at the gifts she gave me.

My mom's path was one of self and family healing. This path led her to become one of the first Westerners to meditate and practice yoga. I remember being a child and waking up to the sweet smell of incense and a feeling of well being mixed in the air with the incense. She practiced transcendental meditation until learning about *vipassana* from our teacher, Annagarika Dhamma Dinna, in Cootney Bay, Canada. One winter my brother, my mother and I made our way together to Cootney Bay for a meditation retreat with Annagarika. It is common for unhealed material to arise in consciousness during meditation retreats. As Mom and I went through the normal emotional upheavals of early retreat practice, we often got pulled down by one another's arisings. I remember my mom talking day and night with Annagarika, eating licorice she had sneaked into the hall and reading, all retreat no-no's. In the callowness of my youth I sat, watched my breath and judged my mother. I rued the day I decided to spend a week on retreat with her. Today I just feel incredibly blessed to have shared that transformative experience with the woman who gave me this precious human life.

At around the age of thirteen, Jewish children are invited to make a personal and public commitment to Judaism. When I was that age my mother was one of the religious school teachers at our temple. One sunny San Fernando Valley afternoon she took me aside and asked me if I wanted to commit to Judaism. I told her that there were too many aspects of Judaism I just could not go along with. She said, okay, if I'm not going to continue on with Judaism, I needed to find an alternate spiritual path. That alone would put my mother into the all time great mothers' and spiritual teachers' hall of fame. But it got even better. I told her that there was a Vedanta Hindu Temple in Hollywood I was interested in. It seems strange that a child that age would be interested in exploring Eastern religions, but I was a dharma nerd from a very early age. My mother drove me each Sunday from the San Fernando Valley all the way to Hollywood to attend services.

When I became a mother, my daughter also benefited from my mother's gifts. Through a divorce, chronic fatigue syndrome, and much psychic cleansing, the spiritual practice fostered by my mother helped me stay present with my daughter. I shudder to think what would have happened to my daughter and me if not for the anchor of spiritual practice. My life is still full of challenges and I continue to grow. I've developed a general appreciation for ALL the beautiful, ugly, wild and tame stuff of life that would not be appreciated without the support of my mother's teachings.

There truly is no way I could ever repay my mom for the gifts she has given. She had plenty of problems and fears, but somehow managed to see the paramount value of spiritual practice through it all. After writing my book, *Buddha Mom*, my life took an unexpected turn. I became a writer and spiritual teacher. Never did I imagine that my mother's direction would lead to my life's work. My mother's gift, my spiritual practice, has not only sustained me through many rough and painful terrains, it has become that which clothes and feeds me. Her wisdom, love and pioneering approach to teaching spirituality to children are the bedrock of my life.

~ *Jacqueline Kramer*

2

Spiritual Lessons of Love

To love deeply in one direction
makes us more loving in all others.

- Anne-Sophie Swetchine

Like Mother, Like Father

Heed the still small voice that so seldom leads us wrong,
and never into folly.
– Marquise du Deffand

My teenage son Eric decided that Mom was a little off her rocker. My stories about remarkable spiritual experiences simply couldn't be true. Although he spent more time with me, his father's "rational" teachings affected his decision-making process more than mine did. I don't know why, but culturally we listen to a man's voice more than a woman's. It didn't take a psychic to know that my ex-husband constantly insinuated to our son that his mother was weird, and purposely set out to teach him that metaphysics was crazy.

It was a challenge for me to remember that my children, as all children, chose their parents for specific soul experiences.

When I'd been pregnant with Eric, I abruptly awoke from a deep sleep one night and saw a ball of golden light above me. I heard a familiar voice telling me that I was going to have a son who would be just like his father. This baby was my son reincarnated from a Native American lifetime that I had first recalled as a little girl of seven when I was sitting by myself in my bedroom closet, pretending to be in a teepee. I was holding my doll close to my heart, wailing deeply in a

Native American language that slipped easily out of my mouth. I felt such strong grief. As I moaned and rocked out my deep sorrow for a past life, my mother stormed into the room and swung open the closet door, "What are you making all that noise about?"

"Mom, I am singing for my husband who died as we made love in the woods. I made so much noise in my joy with him that some white men came along and heard us. They killed him while he was atop of me and then they all raped me! I conceived this baby boy. God says this boy will return to me! I will birth him again!"

Needless to say, that didn't go over well. My mother wanted to know where in God's name I ever got an idea like that. I told her about reincarnation. She screamed, "There is no such thing!"

"Jesus told me about reincarnation! And Great Aunt Gladys, Grandpa's sister, told me we are descended from Chief Pemigewasset!"

"We don't have any proof that we are related to Indians!"

"Aunt Gladys said you would say we weren't related to those damn Indians!" My mother washed my mouth out with soap and took my doll away from me for a day.

Clearly, my ex and I did not parent according to the same goals and expectations. I had married a man, who, like my mother, did not support my inner knowing. It was as if my husband's way of thinking versus my way of thinking was a battleground being fought in our son's consciousness. I wanted Eric to know that both ways of thinking were valid, that he should never give his power away to one or the other hemisphere of his brain. Left-brained, right-brained – the debate of the centuries. It was good to be whole-brained, fully cognizant of all one's senses.

I am a mother and I am psychic. I knew deeply in my soul that my son would not listen to me, so I set up a time to speak with him in the presence of an aunt he trusted in hopes that he would take my words more sincerely into account. "Eric," I said, "I know you don't like what I do, but I have a message for you. In the next ten days, you need to be especially careful. I see an explosion around you. It seems to be caused by something that practically defies nature."

He made small noises and walked away from me across the long log cabin porch. It reminded me of when he was ten months old and bit my nipple while nursing. I gently reprimanded him and he leapt off my lap in a dead run, never to breastfeed again. Now, as he got into his truck to go to his Dad's garage, I asked Eric's aunt, "Do you think he heard me?"

"Can't tell." That was often true with Eric.

Nine days later Eric's grandmother came running through the kitchen door, breathless and weeping hysterically. "Eric was packing a rod in a cannon he made and it exploded! He hadn't even lit it yet. He made the cannon at his Dad's garage from a blueprint off the Internet! Eric is at the emergency room now. He has lost his hand. They're going to airlift him by helicopter to a hospital two hours away that can handle his injuries. Peter says there is nothing that can be done. His hand is gone for good! What will he do?"

I hugged the grief-stricken grandmother, calming her; "Eric has seen me live graciously with a disability for his whole life. He will be fine. Would you please take me to the hospital?" Because of a circulation problem and blood clots in my legs, I can't drive.

I don't remember the ride or walking into the hospital. I just remember being at Eric's head as he lay on the stretcher. I whispered in his ear, "Please ask Archangel Michael for help." He immediately rolled his eyes and told me to stop it.

I begged my ex-husband for a ride to the hospital where Eric was being transferred. "You know I can't drive! How am I supposed to get there?" My ex adamantly refused. A paramedic member of the rescue team overheard me and asked," How much do you weigh?" A hundred and fourteen pounds. "Get in the helicopter." Off I flew with my son.

While Eric was in surgery I sat in the waiting room and went into "psychic" mode. I was clairvoyantly shown a team of angels working with my son. They were telling him that he had a choice: he could leave, or he could stay on earth, but he would have to choose his soul's way. He was shown what that was. I could not see it; only he could. He agreed to stay. The team of angels around him told him about his hand. When he recovered enough for a second surgery, the use of three fingers, minus the thumb and the index finger, would be restored. My son grieved in this altered state but decided to have the courage to survive.

Shortly afterwards, the doctor came out and tapped me on the shoulder, summoning me out of meditation. He told me Eric had gone into respiratory arrest. They had to stop the surgery and put him on a respirator. The shrapnel from the gunpowder had damaged his lungs. That's when I lost it. No amount of metaphysical knowledge could soothe my mother's heart. I couldn't imagine the pain of even thinking about losing Eric. Thankfully, he made it through that crisis.

Over the next six weeks, while I was in the hospital with Eric, I taught him what I knew about being able to survive. If I ever called it metaphysical in nature, his mind would shut down. I learned to deliver the information in a way he found palatable. I had always taught my children to question authority, but I had failed to teach a tool that would have saved my son his hand: *how to know and trust his own knowing*. I had been too wrapped up in my fear of trusting my own inner self.

If only – the two saddest words in the world – *if only* I had said to Eric, "If you get a message from your soul that you need to do something a little differently, please listen to it. It will be a small voice.

It will not shout in your ear. It may even seem silly to make such an adjustment, but trust it."

I later learned that my son had been given a message just prior to the accident. As he was packing the cannon, the voice said, "If you pack this cannon with a different rod, if it does blow, it won't harm you." My son paused for a millisecond, thinking of what I had told him. "Oh, Ma can't be right."

Boom.

Eric recovered from his injuries. Many people came forward to support him and my heart flooded with gratitude. Miraculously, he began engineering college on time. He did physical therapy and trainings two times a day, and came in fifth in the hammer throw for the 2003 Division III Men's Outdoor Track and Field Championship. He remembers to always do his best, no matter what the circumstances, and this makes him a true champion in my eyes. Although he clearly inherited his father's engineering intelligence, his heart and spirit are from the same mold as his mother's.

Do you want the best possible protection for your children? Teach them to recognize and heed their own inner knowing.

~ *Rhobbin Alexis*

A Soul Decision

There are no classes in life for beginners:
right away you are always asked to deal with what is
most difficult.
~ Rainer Maria Rilke

I was in the process of a divorce when it all started. My three children aged 6, 5 and 4 had spent the weekend with their dad. Kyra, my five-year old daughter, walked in the door with tiny purple bruises all over her face. When I asked her what had caused the bruises, Kyra told me she'd been playing baseball and had been hit in the face by a ball. I wondered about the care her father was giving. The next day she went to kindergarten and returned with even more bruises.

Alarmed, I immediately took her to our family physician, Dr. Baird, a wonderful Scottish man. When I told him that all three of my kids, and their cousin had recently had the measles Dr. Baird's eyes lit up. He had the explanation! One in 10,000 people have a complication from the measles which affects the platelets that stop bruising. It was a problem. Dr. Baird told me not to worry and to call him if it became worse.

I'd never been a worrier – always assuming that everything would be okay. Little did I know how much trouble my "Pollyanna" attitude would create.

Two days later, at 5:00 p.m. there was a knock at the front door. I opened it to find a man in a dark overcoat holding a black briefcase and a woman in a dark suit. They were from the Children's Aid Society and told me they wanted to ask me some questions. I invited them in, wondering why they had come. Only later did I find out the school principal had called them.

I led them to the living room. The man sat next to me on the coach and the woman on another. Of course, with visitors in the house, my kids left the TV to join the fun. The woman introduced herself as a nurse and pulled from her briefcase a blank outline of a child's body – front and back view. She began to ask Kyra questions about the bruises. Kyra became excited with all the attention and took off her shirt to show all the tiny bruises on her torso. As I watched the nurse putting "X's" on the body outline, the man began to ask me questions about my divorce. He said he was a psychologist. He asked me if I was lonely or depressed living on my own with three small children. I realized there was no way I could answer – if I said yes, he would think I was beating Kyra, if I said no, he would think I was lying. I could not win.

I gave the explanation Dr. Baird had given me, but the man didn't believe me. When I called Dr. Baird so that he could confirm his explanation regarding Kyra's bruises, he had left the office for the day. The C.A.S. workers told me we would have to go to North York General Hospital for photos and a check-up. There was nothing to do but to agree. I dropped the other two kids at a neighbour's home and left for the hospital.

When we arrived at the Emergency Ward, Kyra was asked to undress while they found a photographer to document the bruising. They clearly suspected me as a child beater. I knew that there was nothing I could say to convince them of my innocence, so while the hospital curtains were closed I dressed Kyra and made a run for the exit. We ran out of the Emergency Ward and thumbed a ride to the home of a friend who promised to hide us from the police until I could talk to my doctor. I called my neighbour and my ex-husband to let them know what had happened and learned that the police had put out a warrant for my arrest and were searching for me.

The next morning Dr. Baird arranged for me to go to a private clinic to have Kyra's blood work done as proof of the measles complication. After the blood sample was taken, Kyra's face was covered in purple bruises. Her blood complication had become an emergency situation. With such a dangerously low platelet level, a simple cut could kill her.

Kyra was sent by ambulance to Sick Children's Hospital. Life as I knew it stopped. At Sick Kids she was given blood transfusions. After two weeks the doctors drew the conclusion that Kyra had cancer and told me to prepare for her death. They said there was nothing more they could do and told me to take her home.

From the time she was very young, Kyra always had a problem with living in this world. She was born a girl, but wanted to be a boy like her older brother. She would even stand to "pee". She refused to wear a dress and she argued and fought and cried every day. As I thought about these things, I realized that Kyra was being forced to make a decision about her life.

Once home, I put her to bed and then told Kyra we needed to talk. I told her she had a choice to make. She could decide to leave this world and her family, or she could decide to live and get better, be a part of her family and agree to be a girl. I told her I loved her very much and wanted her to choose to live, but it was her choice. I told her she had the next five or ten minutes to decide and then she could come out of her room and tell me her decision.

In my church, Eckankar, Religion of the Light and Sound of

God, I had learned that each of us is Soul, not just a physical body. That night I spoke to Kyra, not as the five-year old girl I loved so dearly, but as Soul making a choice about life in this world. I was willing to accept Kyra's choice.

I closed the door to her bedroom and sat down in the living room where I did a spiritual exercise by singing HU, an ancient name for God that opens a channel to the Holy Spirit. I sang this love song to God quietly and asked that whatever was for the good of the whole, I'd be willing to accept. Inwardly, it felt like a huge wash of water flowed over me. It was like a huge wave of an ocean, then all was quiet. I continued to sing HU. Minutes later, I heard Kyra's door open. She walked out of her room and I turned around to face her. She said: "I decided to live".

From that point on Kyra's health improved. The Children's Aid Society apologized for the stress they caused, but said they only had her welfare in mind.

Today, Kyra is a beautiful, 31-year old woman. Her search for truth and life's meaning has taken her to Raanana, Israel, where she practices Orthodox Judaism with her husband and three children. She lives there happily and rarely does she ever wear trousers.

~ *Marlene Chapelle*

You Learn

After a while you learn
the subtle difference between
holding a hand and chaining a soul
and you learn that love doesn't mean possession
and company doesn't mean security.
And you begin to learn that kisses aren't contracts
and presents aren't promises and you begin to accept
your defeats with your head up and your eyes ahead
with the grace of an adult not the grief of a child.
And you learn to build your roads today
because tomorrow's ground is too uncertain for plans
and futures have ways of falling down in mid-flight.
After a while you learn that even sunshine
burns if you get too much so you plant your
own garden and decorate your own soul
instead of waiting for someone to bring you flowers.
And you learn that you really can endure
that you really are strong
and you really do have worth
and you learn
and you learn...
with every goodbye, you learn

~ Veronica A. Shoffstall

A Knowing

"Mommy! I just saw God's spirit flying through the trees!" Quickly, I took my eyes off the road and looked, but saw only the wind waving the feathery branches. I stared at my four-year-old daughter in the rearview mirror. Where did she get this special connection with God, this easy entitlement to see what others spend their lives just trying to believe?

It all started a little before Thanksgiving in the backseat of my car. I was driving to my friend Jody's house to pick up a Pocahontas costume for the school play, since I couldn't sew an Indian dress if my life depended on it. I idled at a crosswalk, waiting for a pedestrian, and heard Julianne singing a sweet song I didn't recognize. Peeking back, I saw her little body completely still, hands clasped like a supplicant in prayer. She looked out the window lost in reverie, singing each word with a loving, familiar caress. When the last note of the melody hung quietly suspended, I asked, "Julianne, is that from the play?"

Her lips curved upwards in an angelic smile. "No, Mommy. It's a lullaby. My other mommy sang it to me when I was in her tummy."

My hands trembled as my world did a half circle around and I fought the desire to pull over the car and take her in my arms. Her birthmother had told me in the hospital that she sang a special lullaby to Julianne during the long months of pregnancy. I glanced back. A dreamy look had settled over Julianne's freckled face; her thoughts on something only she could know.

Thanksgiving melted into Christmas and a few months later, we were again in the car, the fertile chassis for Julianne's revelations, when I asked her, "What was your favorite present from Santa?" I expected her to say the Care Bear, since it never left her sight.

Instead, she whispered softly, "I love the *Polar Express* bell Santa gave me. It has the same sound as the bell I heard when I was in my birth mommy's tummy. So it's really special to me."

Looking back, I recognized that familiar look in those brown eyes, memories locking her thoughts into place, and scattering mine. I had no doubt she was back in her mother's womb again. Shivering in the warm sunlight, I gripped the steering wheel a little harder, trying to hold on to my center of gravity.

Spring bloomed; Julianne turned five and demanded we cut her hair. When we were driving home from the salon, I caught a glimpse of her in the rearview mirror. She looked so beautiful and grown-up, her cropped strawberry-blonde hair gleaming like a halo around her head. I pulled to a stop at a red light and thought of the recent dinner I'd had with my girlfriends.

*   *   *

The waiter had just delivered our pasta when Annie started to complain about a trip to the mall. "It's the colors I see."

"Colors?" Jody asked.

Annie picked up her fork, then put it down, and sighed. "I see people's auras and there's something about the mall that sends them flying at me in a million blinding rays." She pressed her hands around her wine glass. "Gives me a headache."

Jody and I looked at each other, our cheese fondue all but forgotten. I didn't want to make Annie uncomfortable, but now that my daughter had broadened my worldview to include the ether, I had to know more. "Annie," I asked, "can you see our colors?"

She swirled the remainder of her burgundy, downed it, and replied, "Jennifer, you're yellow. Always yellow. Jody, you're green."

That night, I went home and Googled auras. Yellow was sensitive, creative, intellectual, the essence of me. I scrolled through the other colors and found Jody. She was green all right, powerful and intelligent, good in finance. I wondered about Julianne. Reading on, I discovered that many children have pink auras which reflect their compassionate, honest and loving souls. It seemed a perfect composite of Julianne's true nature.

                    *   *   *

The driver behind me honked and, as I accelerated, it occurred to me that if Julianne knew her life in the womb, maybe she, like Annie, could also see what lay beyond my field of vision.

"Honey?"

She mumbled a response, but her gaze didn't shift from the auto mall.

"When you look at Mommy's head and shoulders, do you see a color?"

"Yeah."

Goosebumps pricked. I tried to be casual.

"What color, Julianne?"

Eyes wide, gaping at a huge, obscene Hummer splayed high on a pedestal, she answered without any hesitation, "Yellow."

I tightened my hands on the steering wheel and breathed deeply. Her answer was so matter of fact that it should have been enough, but the intellectual yellow wanted further proof. We started driving up the steep hill that led to our house and saw a neighbor walk quickly into her doorway, arms full of groceries. "Julianne, what about her?" I pointed at the unsuspecting neighbor. "Does she have a color?"

"Yes, Mommy." A bored voice. "She's dark blue, maybe black. Sick."

The minute I got inside my house, I ran to the computer and a quick search revealed that dark blue and black were colors of illness, depression. My fingers froze on the keyboard. Come to think of it, my neighbor hadn't seemed that happy lately.

Later that day the doorbell rang. Julianne shouted out, "Perianne!" and ran to the door to greet her play date. Jody, who had stopped by, coughed and snuffled into a kleenex as the girls started to run towards Julianne's room.

"Wait!" I commanded and they skidded to a stop. "Julianne, remember the color game? What color is Perianne?"

"Pink, Mommy, can we go play now?"

"What about Jody?"

A big grown-up sigh. "Blue, but she's usually green." A "Duh Mom" look. "Come on, Perianne!"

Jody mouthed "Blue?" and I nodded my head, laughing, amazed by Julianne's gift. Now I knew she shared Annie's ability to see through life's paned, cloudy windows into our vibrant energy fields.

After school the next day, Julianne and I walked into our cozy coffee house for a treat. As we stood in line, I wondered what it would be like to see colors around the people in front of me. Did they bother Julianne? Or did she see them as rainbows dancing in the air, fun to watch? I turned to ask her, but she was gone. Whipping around, I saw her making a beeline towards a woman who sat alone, lost in thought, all curled up in a roomy armchair. Before I could stop her, Julianne climbed into the stranger's lap and wrapped her arms around her neck, hugging her tightly as if she were a dear friend. Embarrassed, I ran over to them and started to apologize, but the woman waved a hand at me, tears running down her cheek.

"It's OK," she whispered, holding Julianne close. "I really needed this hug today."

Julianne slid out of the woman's lap and followed me outside to the sidewalk. I tried to take her hand, but she preferred to swing on my arm, making sure to jump on every crack. As we headed next door to Blockbuster, I reminded her that we needed to be careful hugging people we didn't know. She dismissed me like she would an irritating fly buzzing around her ears and ran into the store. I paused inside the door and tried to regain my momentum, wondering if she understood.

We grabbed a video and got in line. Julianne scanned the candy display next to the register, then stopped, and looked up at the man standing behind us. He glanced down, giving her a casual smile. She studied him, her intense gaze begging his attention, making him shift his feet. Suddenly, she threw her arms around him, her little face pressed against his belt buckle. Startled, he stepped back, almost dropping his tapes.

With a stern voice he admonished her, "Don't do that! You don't know me. I'm a stranger!"

She studied him once more, her gaze penetrating and direct. Quietly, she said in an old voice, "I know you. You're a good man."

Astonished, the man and I just stared at each other.

And it was then I knew that my child, who could remember life in her birthmother's womb and see auras, was also a healer who came to bestow love. As her mother, I can only stand back and watch as Julianne follows her path. There is nothing in the sanitized mommy manuals that prepares you to mother a feisty, independent child with spiritual gifts. You just grab her by the coattails, hang on for the ride and in that instant, when she 'knows', you see a glimmering of your own humanity, your own special connection to God.

~ *Jennifer Gay Summers*

She Walks in Beauty

She walks in beauty, like the night
Of cloudless climes and starry skies;
And all that's best of dark and bright
Meet in her aspect and her eyes:
Thus mellow'd to that tender light
Which heaven to gaudy day denies.

One shade the more, one ray the less,
Had half impair'd the nameless grace
Which waves in every raven tress,
Or softly lightens o'er her face;
Where thoughts serenely sweet express
How pure, how dear their dwelling-place.

And on that cheek, and o'er that brow,
So soft, so calm, yet eloquent,
The smiles that win, the tints that glow,
But tell of days in goodness spent,
A mind at peace with all below,
A heart whose love is innocent!

~ *Lord Byron*

Miracle Mom

Here is the test to find whether your mission
on earth is finished:
If you're alive, it isn't.
~ Richard Bach

In May 2002 my Mom was not the woman she is today. She was on a chemo pump, feeling like she wouldn't make it because Esophageal Cancer reared its ugly head. As if the lumpectomy on her breast just two years before wasn't enough, this news had plunged our family into despair once again.

That day my father barely noticed the beauty of the bright spring morning as he drove Mom to Kingston Hospital for her usual radiation treatment. He kept thinking back and worrying about the night before when she kept falling down and couldn't seem to keep her balance no matter how hard she tried.

His fears were confirmed when the doctors said Mom must be admitted to hospital. Her weight had taken a sudden drop and she was considerably weaker than her last visit, just one week before. The chemo, apparently, was too much for this woman of 69 years.

Even though her world was crashing down around her, her spirits had stayed high and she'd tried to keep my father from worrying.

He had come to know that it was his turn now to be the caregiver, after all those years she had taken care of him. Offers of help from the four children had been turned down and he committed himself fully to her care.

That night when my phone rang at 7:00 pm, my father's deep voice gave away his concern. "Victoria," he said, "your mother has been admitted to the hospital. It seems her chemo pump is too much for her and they are sorting it all out now."

"Dad, Dad," I started to cry, "Let me drive there right now! Please don't shut me out. I am worried she isn't going to make it. I can tell by your voice that you're worried and I need to be with my Mommy!"

"Your mother will be fine. She is only here for tests to regulate the pump. She is in isolation and you won't be allowed in to see her anyway. Don't try to drive here. In the state you're in, you'll end up in an accident. You won't be able to help anyone that way Vicki."

After hanging up, I fell to the floor crying. I knew it was much more than routine tests. My Mom was like no other Mom; she was my best friend. We had an amazing connection that was the envy of my friends in high school. She always knew everything about me without me even saying a word. We felt we had been together before in many lifetimes and she and I talked about that a great deal as I was raising my own children.

My emotions had been all over the place when my Mom first fell ill and with the more recent developments I found myself constantly shaking all over. I didn't think I could live without my Mom.

Still crumpled on the floor in tears, I felt a gentle rubbing on my back. It was my eight year old daughter comforting me and saying everything would be okay. She didn't know the details, but she knew something big was happening. I stood up, hugged her and in my grief started to scream over her head, "MOM, MOM, MOM please don't leave me! Mom you can't go! I need you so much…PLEASE DON'T GO! PLEASE MOM, DON'T GO!"

I have no idea the time that passed as I kept asking out loud for my Mom to stay on earth. Eventually my husband came home and I told him my mother might end up in Heaven with his Mom this very night. I couldn't sleep at all. I just kept asking her, begging her not to leave me!

Miraculously, that night Mom did improve. Her vital signs and her blood pressure came back and the doctors were amazed that she had survived.

The survival rate for esophageal cancer, we're told, is 5-10% and this 69 year old little bit of a woman came back from it fighting – and fighting hard.

Only two days later the drive to my childhood home felt like five hours instead of two. I went there alone to be with the woman that helped mold the person I am today. I was so grateful that God didn't take her that night. I knew he thought about it and I thanked him for letting me have more time with her.

I remember creeping in the back door of my parent's home. I didn't look for my father, but went straight to Mom. She was lying on the couch. I looked at her and saw the woman who brought me the spirituality I live everyday: the woman who is my heart and soul. I touched her forehead and brushed her hair from her eyes and I silently cried.

She was very lucid and looked at me with her electric blue eyes. "Vicki, I saw the light. There was a bright, bright light honey, surrounded with beautiful pinks and reds. They took me to a school room and showed me I would need to learn more. It was an old school house, all pine and oak. The colors in the school room were like I have never seen. It was so peaceful."

"Victoria, I would have stayed there, but all I could hear was you yelling at me. Your voice was screaming, 'Mom, don't leave me, Mom, don't leave me!' I cannot see the man's face Vicki but I asked him if I could have more time back on Earth because I have a great deal of forgiving to do."

I knew at that moment that all I believed about God and miracles was true. I put my hands together and I thanked Him.

It is May 2006 and I just got off the phone with Mom. We talked about this story and how it always sends chills through us. We remember the forgiveness she needed to feel and how everyday is special to us now.

Since that night doctors crowd around her and treat her like a Queen because they say she is a walking miracle. They journal her each and every visit and I bet they talk about her on their golf courses. My Mom was always a miracle to me, but now the rest of the world knows too.

~ *Vicki Bruce*

My Mother's Old Soul

We cannot live for ourselves alone. Our lives are
connected by a thousand invisible threads, and along
these sympathetic fibers, our actions run as causes
and return to us as results.
~ Herman Melville

My mother was born in Poland, after World War II, to a German mother and a Jewish father. Even as an infant, she became known as an "old soul". It all began when the town's oldest and wisest woman saw my grandparents with their baby. The old woman looked at the baby, my mother, and said, "In your blood line you carry a lot of ancient grief and disharmony, but your old soul, like the summer's sun will outshine that by bringing healing, loving kindness, peace and above all, hope to all that will come in contact with you."

In time my mother got married and had two daughters while she was very young herself. When we were small children my father escaped what was, back then, a poverty stricken, spiritually intolerant, communistic country. His plan was to someday bring his family to join him in Canada.

Several years later my grandmother was diagnosed with ovarian cancer. Shortly afterward, she underwent a complete hysterectomy.

This resulted in ongoing serious infections and dramatic weight loss. The doctors said her prognosis for recovery was very poor. All of this left my grandfather devastated and he became very depressed, unable to cope, or to run his family business.

Strangely, all this made my mother more energetic and hopeful. In our eyes, my sister's and mine, she transformed her quiet and peaceful soul to that of a brightly burning fire. She ceaselessly cared for her ailing mother, giving her the best natural remedies, singing to her and giving her powerful words of hope. She attended to the household chores, continued the family business and helped to organize food deliveries to the elderly and less fortunate in the community.

My sister and I hadn't seen that side of her before. We were awestruck by her healing energy. Somehow she still reserved, as we called it, "magic time", which meant she would either take us on "park exploration walks" or treat us to "hugs-time", when she would read to us or tell us beautiful stories. Throughout the ordeal of her mother's illness and her dad's withdrawal, her old soul shone brightly.

Two months passed and to the astonishment of all, my grandmother completely recovered. Grandfather became cheerful again and resumed his business. It seemed like a miracle when soon after, my mother, sister and I were granted permission to go to Canada where my father had set up a home for us.

Its was if the Divine rewarded my mother for her acts of sacrifice and compassion. My sister and I even thought that our mother possessed some kind of magic.

Being new immigrants to Canada, we were very poor and felt like strangers in another world. Our arrival was during a recession and our father found it hard to find steady work. Our mother was unfazed by the challenge of all this and her light started to shine again. She quickly found a factory job which involved working nights and enduring hard labor. Unlike her co-workers, she worked with enthusiasm, as if she owned the business. This dedication was noticed by her managers and she was promoted and given more authority. Some co-workers became jealous of my mother, but she recognized that there must be some personal hurt behind these jealousies and rather than reacting, she reached out in empathy, to bring positive thought and hope. She knew that competition and jealously can kill the human spirit, but kindness and compassion can heal it.

When the two of us became teenagers, my sister was allured by the status of the "rebellious in-crowd" and started hanging out with two girls who were into drugs, stealing and who were generally unmotivated by school and learning. I couldn't understand why, but every time my sister brought these two girls over to our house, my mom went out of her way to befriend them. My mother said to me, "Every person has a beautiful guiding light inside them. You just have to help that person find it and that light will do its own magic." To my surprise, after about six months of interacting with my mother, these girls were somehow different. They lost their rebelliousness and in its place there was peaceful focus.

Many years later, after my sister and I had moved out of our parents' house, I ran into one of these girls, now a woman. She told me that she had married and was working as a preschool teacher. Just before saying our good-byes, she said "I just wanted to let you know something about your mom. I never met such a kind and helpful person. I really believe that it was no coincidence that she was there when my life could have turned down the wrong path. There is something beyond words about her. Her kindness and spirit really spoke to me."

There are many other wondrous works of my mother's old soul, but to tell them all would fill this entire book. The real beauty of life is often experienced through the great spirits we encounter. We seldom take the time to appreciate their positive force in our lives. They may even be our own mothers. They are right there ready and waiting to teach us about hope and love, to show us the beautiful spirit in ourselves and in others. No matter how busy our lives get, it is important to take a moment to look into our mothers' hearts and be in awe of their ever loving and uniquely precious spirits.

~ *Joanna Kokalovski*

Smart Food

Paul was in trouble again. The incidents at school were escalating with his bad behavior. His teacher, who taught kindergarten to grade two in our small school, was new to the profession and assured me that it was normal for young boys to be impulsive. I learned that a smaller boy had been promising Paul rewards if he would kick or punch other kids. Getting caught didn't seem to matter because Paul liked being physical.

Paul also had difficulties with his speech, pronouncing his "R's" like "W's" causing him frustration when people couldn't understand him. Because of this, he began to develop a bad temper and destroyed most of his toys. By the time he reached grade three, he was involved in fights behind the school. His peers began talking about guns and violence. Hunting was common in our community and they would often talk about shooting bears, or each other or themselves. This was a big wake-up call.

It was during this time that a new teacher called me in for a meeting. I was alarmed when told Paul was two years behind in reading and was having difficulty with writing. If we didn't change our strategy, he would keep falling behind. His strengths were his sense of humor, brilliant and fast-moving mind, and curiosity about the inner workings of things. But reading and writing were holding him back.

When it came time for homework, he couldn't concentrate. I

needed to find out how I could help him. Already health conscious because of health issues I'd encountered some years prior, I began researching the effects of certain foods on the body and learned that essential fatty acids (EFA's) were necessary for brain function. Deficiencies could lead to learning difficulties; more than 80% of North Americans do not get enough in their diet. When I approached my doctor about this, he informed me that boys need more EFA's than girls and it was difficult to get enough through foods like green lettuce, fish and seeds. He told me to try giving him a supplement of oils like tuna or flax oil and that it would take about six weeks to see any changes. Paul hated the taste, even though we tried everything we could to disguise it such as putting it in fruit juice and making Popsicles. He complained about having to take it, but after a while, he knew he had no choice.

About six weeks later, I noticed that Paul was sitting on the floor quietly doing his homework. He looked as though he was enjoying it and wasn't complaining! I was thrilled. We worked hard that whole year. Paul read out loud every night and did many pages of reading responses for comprehension. He worked on his typing and worked hard to improve his handwriting. We also played games provided by his speech therapist as often as possible and finally had some success. He still complained – especially about taking the oils – but I never let up on the discipline, trying to make the work as fun as possible, buying him his favorite comics as rewards, and after a while it became part of his routine

Paul's behavior began to improve as well. He still wanted to belong, but something was changing within him. He began to care and became more conscious of how his actions affected others. He now had the strength to say no when asked to do things he didn't want to do – and had the confidence to know who his friends were.

With his new attitude, Paul became a positive role model for others, in one instance leading his best friend away from wrong doing.

I was overjoyed, when at the end of grade three Paul won the "Most Improved Student" award. Over the next few years, he continued to take pride in his work. Now in Grade 8, he is pulling A's and B's in every subject and is a wonderful role model for the younger students at recess and during extra curricular activities. He has told me how much he now appreciates the help I gave him and is happy to be doing so well at school. He is even saving money for his university education and hopes to be an Aerospace Engineer. I know he can do it!

~ *Shari Tallon*

The Road Less Traveled

Do not follow where the path may lead.
Go instead where there is no path and leave a trail.
- Ralph Waldo Emerson

As I stood before my brother's coffin, wanting so desperately to understand why he had taken his life, I made a promise to him that his death would not be in vain. Standing there, weeping in disbelief, I made a vow to my eight year-old son David that he would not inherit the legacy of alcoholism that had brought so much grief to my family, my brother and myself.

I was born in the spring of 1952, the first of five children, in the small mining town of Timmins, Ontario, Canada. In the late fall of 1953, I was still too young to know that my father was a chronic alcoholic and that my Mother, at her wits end, had decided to take me and leave my father. She presented him with an ultimatum; stop drinking or we are gone. Not wanting to lose his precious baby girl, he quit drinking and joined the fellowship of Alcoholics Anonymous. Our home became an unofficial treatment center, our lives revolving around alcoholics and Alcoholics Anonymous.

And so my life was a series of mishaps and misfortunes, highlighted by sexual abuse and addiction. Finally at eighteen-years-old,

I left my family and moved to North Bay to attend College. While there, I met Fred, who was stationed in North Bay with the Armed Forces. I was in love for the first time, so desperately in love. Fred and I were married on June 29, 1974 and two years later on January 7th, 1976, our only son, David, was born.

Children learn what they live, and I didn't want my son to grow up the way I had, so about five years into the marriage I started going to Alcoholics Anonymous. My Mom was drinking very heavily at the time and it was taking a tremendous toll on the emotional and mental health of our family, individually and collectively. I didn't want to have this legacy of alcoholism continue another generation. It had gone on for four, if not five, generations that I knew of.

On June 29th, 1984, our ninth wedding anniversary, I went strawberry picking with David in the morning and then to the Gatineau Hills for a picnic and swimming. It was a beautiful sunny day and I felt incredibly blessed and lucky to be alive. We arrived home at four p.m. to a call from my brother, Jim, who'd apparently been trying to reach me all day. He was hysterical as he said, "Dougie's dead. He's committed suicide!"

I thought, 'Stop it. That's not funny.' Douglas was only seventeen, a very gentle soul and more like a son to me than a brother.

Douglas's death acted like an atomic bomb for my family. There was fallout everywhere. Up until then my sheer willpower had kept my marriage together. Now forced to deal with my real feelings, my marriage began to fall apart.

After the funeral, I recognized the signs that I was headed for a "drinking binge" and entered St Joseph's Drug and Alcohol Treatment Centre, while Fred, who had returned from Alert, North West Territories, stayed to look after David. Intensive treatment began as I really began to understand how alcoholism had held me captive.

After I completed my treatment, I returned home to my life still extremely fragile. And then six months later, we were posted across Canada to Calgary, a place where I knew no one. I was drowning in grief and looking for a sign from God.

On Pentecostal Sunday, as I sat in church looking up at the banner of the dove of Pentecost, everything seemed to vaporize except the DOVE – no more people or church or pews. Then to my surprise a voice inside me clearly said, "You must leave your marriage!"

I recoiled at the words and said, "No, I can't. It is too much to ask of me."

I'd known for some time that my marriage was in trouble, but I thought with just a bit more time and effort I could make it work.

The voice was insistent "You must leave your marriage!"

I said I would agree but that HE, the voice, would have to promise to change me, because I knew that if I stayed the same, I would repeat the same mistakes. I left church completely devastated. All that day I cried, until I could cry no longer. Not knowing what to do, Fred went out and took David with him. By the time he returned, I had gained the strength to tell him that I had to leave the marriage. The next day I bought airplane tickets for David and myself to Ottawa, where I had an AA sponsor I trusted, and an AA network of meetings and friends.

At the end of the week, when it was time to leave, I had the heart-wrenching task of explaining to our eight-year-old son what was to happen. Sitting on the rocking chair, I placed David on my lap and looking into his innocent face, I told him how much Mommy and Daddy loved him, but that Deborah and Fred didn't get along any more and that I was going back to Ottawa. I told him it was up to him and that he could choose with whom he wanted to stay. Afterward I regretted giving him that choice. Next came the terrible words, "I am staying with my Daddy." It came as a total shock that my little boy wouldn't be coming to live with me!

I left the house with Fred and David crying on the sidewalk. Stunned and in shock, I somehow got myself to the airport to catch my flight. Sitting on the plane, I kept waiting for someone to sit down beside me, but then I would remember that David wouldn't be accompanying me.

I arrived in Ottawa where a friend from AA was waiting at the airport. Seeing I was alone, she asked, "Where is David?" Again the shock hit me that "My baby is gone."

For the next three months I stayed with a generous AA family to begin my healing. For the first while, I cried, took walks, and went to meetings, just trying to make sense of all that I was feeling. At times, on my walks, my knees would buckle as I collapsed from the weight of my sorrow.

As I progressed in my healing, I moved out of my friend's home, first into one room in a home, then into a basement apartment. That first summer David visited me. I was so happy to see my little boy. But as the years passed my opportunities to see my son were fewer and fewer.

For the first two years I had low paying jobs, busing and waiting tables and working for a medical lab. With the funds from my work, I started accumulating enough to have basic furniture. At one point I decided to apply for a security job. As part of the process, my fingerprints would need to be taken at the Police Station. While there, I heard my Inner Voice say, "Go and apply for a job in dispatch." That made sense to me because I'd worked as a switchboard operator for the Canadian Embassy in Washington DC from 1976 to 1979, when my husband was posted there with the Armed Forces.

The dispatch position was designated as a bilingual, so when I asked for an application form, the Human Resources officer refused after learning I didn't speak French. "Who's looking out for us Englishmen?" I spoke up with resolve, in a way completely out of character for me.

It seemed to have the right affect because the man, who happened to have a thick British accent, brought me into his office and handed me an application for Special Constable, a position that had been brought into existence in 1984. To my amazement and excitement, out of fifteen hundred applicants, I was one of only nine hired! And, although I was afraid of confrontation, I took the job. I knew in my heart that the God of my understanding wanted me in this job for a reason.

Just before I was hired to the Police force, I joined a wonderful religion called Eckankar that taught about divine love and how to master one's own destiny. With tip money from my job waiting tables, I saved enough to fly to Atlanta, Georgia where there was an Eckankar seminar – a congregation of over 5,000 people coming together for spiritual renewal. This was to be a turning point in my healing.

While on a bridge in Atlanta, I was crying as I had been doing for a very long time. A woman passing by stopped and came over to comfort me. I learned she was also a member of Eckankar and coincidently lived in Ottawa too. This was a meeting, soul to soul.

After I returned home, my new friend Jean would call me on the phone to say hello. For many years I never called her back, but that never deterred her from calling to ask how I was and to offer words of encouragement and love.

Jean would call and say, "Deb, I just want you to know that I care. Call me back if you want, just know it's OK if you don't." Over the years a bond of trust grew between us and I started to return her calls. I had finally met someone who loved me unconditionally and never withdrew her love. She broadened my horizons by introducing me to creative people who were spiritual, knowledgeable and expansive. Jean was my lifeline. She always made sure that I didn't stay under too long.

Jean was also instrumental in introducing me to a psychiatrist who opened up a whole new world for me. Through him I got the medication I needed that changed the color of my world from dull gray to all colors of the rainbow. After two years of seeing him I had lost the extra fifty pounds I'd carried most of my life. I was finally letting down my defenses.

Last week I had a dinner party, the first one since my brother's death twenty years ago. I held the party in my own home with freshly painted walls, a new rug and curtains, great food and wonderful friends. A new cycle has begun for me where I am truly experiencing myself as a person worthy of love, joy and happiness.

My son, David, has grown into a wonderful, well-adjusted man and has come to understand why I chose to leave those many years ago. Seeing him grow has helped me realize that I made the right choice back then. David has found the love of his life and I'll be flying out to be present when he says his wedding vows next spring. A big part of my healing came when I read this wonderful letter he wrote to me as a Christmas gift last year.

Dear Mom:

Forgiveness seems to be a trivial thing sometimes, but it is the basis of true unconditional love. I know that only the individual can be responsible for his own feelings. I understand that you must love yourself before you can truly and totally love another. I did not, however, know this from the beginning. It was handed down to me, as are all great bits of wisdom. My teacher is the incredible person I have the honor of calling my mother, who through her own trials and tribulations, came to these same realizations.

I look at myself today, and think of where I am, and can honestly say that I do not think that I would be here if it were not for Deborah Davis, my mom. I have her to thank for my respect of women, for my willingness to take the more difficult route, my not being afraid to express myself to an individual for whom I care, and the stubbornness to never quit. If only Deborah could look at me, the wonderful individual she says I am, and realize that it is only because of her that I possess many of these qualities.

Love, David Russell

These gifts are the light side of the shadow side of my life. I kept my promise to myself and to David. I took the road less traveled and for that I am forever grateful!

~ *Deborah Davis*

Queen of Hearts

I'll ask the wind to breathe a droplet
From Juan de Fucca Straight
over the mountains across the continents
to your door
a servant offering an assortment of velvet shoes
where will you place the treasures
offered you
in the dark of night?

Does eternity look easy
when carried like a Queen
to a mountain top
overlooking your vast empire
knowing no thing is missing
knowing
rainbows begin here?

~ Jean Versteeg

Forgiveness and the General

"But, "*moth-er!*" Those of you who are parents have heard this many times. Before you give in to your teenager's request, are you sufficiently prepared to forgive the consequences? Teaching teens tough lessons is an act of love.

When my daughter was almost sixteen, my Christmas present to my husband was a weekend away for fun, sun, rest, relaxation, and romance during February when northern California weather is at its dreariest. My gift included airline tickets nonstop to Palm Springs, a rented convertible, a bottle of champagne, and two nights at a glorious French Chateau on Lake La Quinta. I made arrangements for our daughter to spend the weekend with friends, which upset her terribly. Heather felt we *should* trust her to stay at home alone. She had always been a very responsible young lady, and she expected us to have confidence in her to be alone for two days. As Mom, I wanted her to be safe and supervised. We explained that there had been several local incidents where teens threw raucous parties while their parents were out of town. We didn't want Heather to find herself in an unpleasant situation she couldn't handle, despite her best intentions. She thought my line of reasoning was ridiculous.

Talks remained heated for weeks. As she and I walked our baby lamb together at night, we discussed trust and responsibility. Mostly I just listened to her pleas. She told me what a very busy weekend she was planning while we were gone. She would need numerous changes of clothes for her various activities, plus she had to be home to feed and care for our barnyard full of animals. "Why can't I just stay in my own home?" she implored. "You are locking me out of my life! I'll have to pack my entire closet and still make a trip everyday to tend to the animals. If you trust me, you'll let me stay home." Her reasoning seemed sound, and I was truly considering her request. Thank goodness my intuition prevailed.

On that long-anticipated Friday in February, my husband and I locked the house and left for what we knew would be a magical weekend. Both of us were really ready for a great weekend away from home as we picked up our convertible and drove to the beautiful inn on the lake. Our pleasure turned to anxiety when Heather phoned early the next morning. Between sobs, she explained that she was okay. However, an unauthorized party had taken place in our yard the previous night. About two hundred teenagers had arrived uninvited and in the pouring rain, started a bonfire. Between the drinking and the brawls, our property had sustained substantial damage to the ponds, lawn, flowerbeds, and outdoor lighting. We were in shock and didn't know how to react. We tried to gather all the facts, but quickly realized that there are always three sides to every story: yours, mine, and the truth.

The *good* news was that no one had been hurt and our animals were all fine. The bad news was that our private space had been invaded, and we had no idea what awaited us at home. We put our cell phones into overdrive, contacting neighbors, friends, and police for more information. Our vacation was ruined. We were angry with our daughter for revealing that we were away and furious with the disrespect of the local teenagers.

Because I believe that there is a reaction for every action, I kept wondering what the lesson in this frustrating event was supposed to be. I was too disappointed and enraged to imagine anything positive. As we hurriedly left for the airport, the proprietors of the inn suggested that perhaps this was going to be an exercise in forgiveness.

Forgiveness is extraordinarily difficult when you are mad and sad, yet I realized that they were right. I needed to forgive. However, I also needed to be a responsible parent. Back home, after conversing with Heather, I telephoned as many parents as possible to inform them of the unauthorized, unchaperoned teen gathering that their child had attended. I met with the school principal and police to discuss arranging chaperoned teen parties in the future and wrote articles in the local papers seeking solutions.

I was truly upset and disappointed with Heather for allowing this assemblage to occur on our property. Heather came home from school a few days after the incident announcing that students had nicknamed me "Sergeant Cynthia" because I took proactive measures in a situation where other parents merely suggested that "teens will be teens". "Sergeant", I exclaimed, "I am not a Sergeant, I'm a General! This is NOT a parent popularity contest. I care about the safety of all of you. My job title is 'Mom', not 'friend.'" Being a loving parent means having the courage to set boundaries, and follow through with appropriate consequences consistently, regardless of what others think.

Heather took full responsibility for allowing the party to occur. She was genuinely remorseful and accepted the repercussions of her actions, patiently enduring our restrictions while she paid off the damages. In turn, we forgave her for this lapse in judgment. Because of this incident, the ramifications that followed, and the gift of forgiveness, our relationship became stronger and more open.

Today, those teens are in college and seek me out for advice and camaraderie. As we laugh about the wild times of high school, they thank me for being the mother who cared enough for their health, safety, and welfare to brave being called Sergeant Cynthia. And most importantly, Heather appreciates me for being the General who could forgive, forget, and forge ahead. We are best friends.

We can't change the past, but we can create a joyous future through forgiveness.

~ *Cynthia Brian*

3

On Losing a Loved One

The love that once was born cannot die
For it has become part of us, of our life,
Woven into the very texture of our being.
Each of us would wish to leave some part of ourselves,
So here and now we bear witness to the one
we knew in life,
Who now in death bequeaths a subtle part,
precious and beloved,
Which will be with us in truth and beauty,
In dignity and courage and love
To the end of our days.

~ Algernon Black

An Everlasting Farewell

My mother, Alicia Jane Phinn, was born on the eleventh day of the first month of the new twentieth century. Daughter of an Irish mother and a United Empire Loyalist father, she carried in her bones the determination to face her own conflicts, find her own truth, and live her own life. Inured to hardships in the pioneer life of Ontario winters and immigrant loneliness, Alicia found her own voice singing for soldiers during the First World War and for the veterans who languished in military hospitals when the fighting was over. The raw horror of that war burned in her eyes and voice when she sang, "There's a silver lining through the dark clouds shining." Her own brother had been a pilot in that war, when planes were new and "splashed on the ground like buttermilk."

Every Sunday night when my father was with his congregation at the church, my two brothers and I sat with our mother around our piano singing war songs, holding back the tears.

At eighteen, Alicia decided to become a nurse. Knowing her parents would reject her stepping out of her home, she bought a trunk and prepared her uniforms, caps and cape for her profession. Her parents got wind of her plan, forbade her leaving home, and gave her a job in a new thriving family business.

Early twenties was the era of the Flappers. With her own money, she bought stylish clothes, a Packard car, dared to be the first to bob her hair, became the soloist in her church, all within the restrictions of her family home.

When my father Andrew, a handsome young minister, arrived in Askin Street Church to preach his ordination sermon, soloist and minister looked into each other's eyes, and knew they had found their destiny. Not an easy destiny for either.

Mother, a young woman with classy shoes, classy hats, classy dresses and bobbed hair, drove into a small town in her own Packard car and found herself hated by all the mothers who hoped Andrew would choose his bride from among their daughters.

When we (my new presence did nothing to ease her outcast state) moved to another town, her first task was to persuade my father to help her return the mattresses, couches and stuffed chairs to the barn where they had come from that afternoon when the Ladies Aid was preparing the furnished parsonage for the new minister. Mother faced them when they arrived that evening to see if everything was fine.

"No," she said. "I am not used to sleeping with mice, nor with a ragged Union Jack for a tablecloth." A new bed arrived the next morning, but that was the repeated narrative of my mother's history with Ladies Aides. She fought to live her own style and her own values.

Often as we washed dishes together, she would suddenly stop, put down the sponge, fasten her hands on the sink, and gaze out somewhere beyond the window and say, "Marion, what do you think is out there beyond the clouds?" I would be struck by her beauty, pale skin, blue eyes, Irish curly hair. I felt her prison. I cried her tears alone.

The depression in the thirties bound our family into deeper dependence on each other. I now had two younger brothers and my mother had developed glandular tuberculosis from tubercular cows. For many months the congregation was unable to pay my father's small salary.

I don't remember deprivation so much as the fun we had together collecting nuts – hickory, beech, walnuts- for the winter; every thanksgiving picking cherries, strawberries, peaches, freezing or canning them. But it was hard work. My mother's condition became serious. A lump the size of an egg developed on her neck. The doctors told her they could cut it out, but she would loose the nerves on one side of her face. She would never smile again. We three children sat in silence and terror while our parents discussed what to do. (We all knew well enough what death was because the graveyard was close at hand. Our mother there!) Mother stood up, "Andrew," she said, "put some boiling water in that bowl." She brought a five-inch darning needle, sterilized it in the boiling water, and stuck it deep into the lump in her neck. Green oozed out with noxious odors. Intuitively, she had guided that needle around arteries, veins, nerves and hit her mark. From that moment I knew she would live.

These stories are essential to understand the healing, the mighty gift my mother gave me forty years later. Age was wearying her; her life-partner was gone. Stronger glasses were needed and a hearing aid. Frequently, she would phone, "Marion, that poem your father used to quote, something about 'Farewell Brutus,' can you quote it for me?" And she would write down poem after poem that she loved.

When I returned from my studies in Zurich in the summer of 1975, I realized how unwell she was. Together we went to several homes for the aged, where we saw only too clearly what lay ahead. Her proud spirit rebelled when a helpful aide pinned a pink bow in her hair and called her "Dearie." She said nothing, but I felt her ultimate '*No*'.

When we returned to the car she said, "You will never put me in a home. Promise me that."

"I promise," I said.

When Ross, Mother and I were on our way to the airport the following October as I was returning to Zurich, I knew in a flash that we would never go to the airport again together.

"I won't go, Mother," I said. "You need me here."

"Marion, if you can be free, go."

And forty-five years of our history together passed before my eyes. The freedom she fought for, the consciousness she so desperately sought, she was giving to me.

One month later, Ross phoned me in Zurich. "I'm in the hospital with your Mother. Here she is."

"Mother I'll be on the next plane. We will have tea together tomorrow night."

"Wouldn't that be lovely," she said. I knew instantly that tea was out of the question.

On the plane I dozed. I felt myself going up a canyon, following my glowing Mother who was going ahead with a lamp lighting my difficult way. I followed for some time, then had to concentrate on the sharp rocks. When I looked up for the light, it was gone. My body convulsed, scattering everything on my tray. Unconsciously I knew my Mother was dead. Consciously I did not accept it.

On arrival at the airport, I asked Ross to drive instantly to the hospital.

"She's gone," he said. I knew it, but it took months to know it.

Later in my despair, I said to him, "She could have waited. People can stay until their loved ones reach them to say good-bye. Why did she choose to go before I arrived?"

"Your mother chose her death," he said. "She said to me, 'I lived for my father, for my husband, for my children. This death is mine. If I'm here when Marion arrives, she'll care for me. I'll be a vegetable. She won't return to Zurich. This will take about two hours.'

Those were her last words. She began her journey into light. At the moment she died, my body convulsed on the plane.

The immensity of her gift to me – BE FREE – is etched into my soul.

When Ross and I went to her apartment, we found the poems I had quoted pinned inside her petticoat, so they would be immediately available to her.

Among them, "*Therefore our everlasting farewell take: For ever, and for ever, farewell, Cassius! If we do meet again, why, we shall smile; If not, why then, this parting was well made.*

~ *Marion Woodman*

Do Not Stand at My Grave

Do not stand at my grave and weep
I am not there; I do not sleep.
I am a thousand winds that blow,
I am the diamond glints on snow,
I am the sun on ripened grain,
I am the gentle autumn rain.
When you awaken in the morning's hush
I am the swift uplifting rush
Of quiet birds in circled flight.
I am the soft stars that shine at night.
Do not stand at my grave and cry,
I am not there; I did not die.

~ Mary Elizabeth Frye

My Mother's Last Gift

All healing is essentially the release from fear.
~ A Course in Miracles

My mother's name was Lillian, and she was the worst negative thinker in the world. Her life was very difficult. She grew up in a little border town between Poland and Lithuania, and when the Nazis came they killed off the whole family. Other than her father and herself, her whole family perished in the Holocaust.

That experience killed off my mother's faith. She often said, "If there is a loving God in the universe, then Holocausts don't happen, little babies don't die, and bad things don't happen to good people." She just sort of gave up. The way she dealt with her pain was to say, "I won't examine my life."

There were two things she taught me as a child. "Number one," she communicated clearly was, "Thou shalt not ever study psychology. If you get in touch with your pain, it will swallow you up." That was how she dealt with it, one foot after the other. The other thing she said was, "Whatever you do, don't study any religions other than Judaism." She didn't think there was anything interesting in Judaism anyway, but at least it was safe.

"Religion," she said, echoing Karl Marx, "is the opiate of the people. It is some kind of line you feed yourself to give meaning to an existence that's intrinsically meaningless." You'd think this kind of thinking would have killed her off quickly. But no, she lived to be 82, and that after a lifetime of smoking and drinking as well. This woman had cast-iron genes.

Lillian and I did not get along well. During the last year of her life, we had often tried to talk about something with substance. I looked often at my relationship with my mother and father as part of my own healing. For years I had carried a great deal of anger about my mother. My chief definition of myself was not as "Joan," but rather, as "not Lillian." Whoever she was, I wanted to be different. That's about the most grievous form of attachment in non-forgiveness that I can think of. It kept me totally out of connecting with my own self, and with what my own life meant.

The healing for that has been a long road. But my mother's death in itself provided a remarkable healing, as well.

The day she died, she had developed some internal bleeding. She was already in hospital, and at nine that morning they took her down to nuclear medicine for some tests. At four in the afternoon, she had not yet returned to her room which, by now, was filled with her friends and relatives who had come to say goodbye. Concerned, they said, "Joan, she's going to die alone on a stretcher somewhere out there unless you go get her." So, I put on my white coat, and resolutely made my way to nuclear medicine. When I found her, she was lying there all alone on a stretcher. She had been there all day. Something had happened. There had been an accident, an emergency, so they let her wait.

I was very upset. Under these circumstances, you really have to assert yourself. Don't let them take your loved ones away without a second thought. I looked at the doctor and said, "This won't do. We have to have her back." And the doctor replied, "I'm sorry, we need a diagnosis."

My mother, always the joker said, "Aahhh! That's why I've been lying here all day? Why didn't you ask me?

The startled doctor said, "What?"

And my mother replied, "I'm dying. There's your diagnosis."

And so I got her out of there. To return her to her room, they needed to put her in an elevator large enough for the stretcher and one other person, the orderly. So the orderly said, "You'll have to meet her in her room."

"No," I said, "I don't," and then I kicked him out of the elevator. This is against hospital rules. You're not allowed to wheel your own family member around. God forbid, something could happen.

Alone in the elevator, she looked at me, knowing this might be our last chance ever to say anything. "Joan, I have to complete this with you," she said. "I know I've made a lot of mistakes. I know it and I'm sorry. Can you forgive me?"

Hearing those words was wonderful. But even more wonderful was that I now had the chance to acknowledge all the mistakes I had made, not by making a list, but just by feeling the feeling. My mother was not interested in long emotional lists. That wasn't her style.

But I did have a list. I was sorry we had never been friends; that I couldn't be there for her as often as I would have liked to; that I had held her in judgment, and most of all I was sorry I had kept her out of my heart. But, just being able to look her in the eyes and say, "Can you forgive me for the mistakes I have made?"

And having her say, "Yes," provided the healing of a lifetime. It was truly amazing.

When I got her back to the room, everyone had gone for a cup of coffee. With the short time left, I looked at her and said, "How about we exchange soul qualities?" Now, this was not the sort of woman with whom one exchanged soul qualities, but in this great moment of openness she said, "Oh sure, I'd love to."

And so I began; "What I've always admired about you was your courage and that you've had tremendous fortitude no matter what." I tend to crumble when the going gets tough.

She said, "I'll give you that." Then she said, "What I would like from you is compassion." The fact that she could even see that in me, that I could be compassionate to everybody else but her, was most amazing.

Some hours later, my twenty-year-old son, Justin, arrived. He was very close to his grandparents. Over the years he had spent a lot of time with my mother. She often babysat him when he was little.

Most of that night, he lay in bed and held her. We said prayers to her and sang everything you could think of. Finally, about three in the morning, she was asleep. Justin and I were sitting on opposite sides of the bed, and I was meditating. It was then I had the vision.

I have had only one vision. It was definitely not a dream. It was very different from a dream. All I can say is it was much more real than this level of reality. The old Tibetans say that we are dreaming now. This life is the substance of a dream. When we leave this life is when we actually wake up.

In this vision, I was a pregnant woman, giving birth to a baby. My consciousness was somehow present in both places. I was both the pregnant mother and the baby.

Then I was a baby being born experiencing a terrible dark night of the soul. I was dying. I was dying to the world of the womb, being born to a whole new life. I was being born, coming through the birth canal and out of the darkness into the most resplendent light. In that moment of birth I suddenly knew everything about my relationship with my mother, all knowledge, right there.

When I opened my eyes, the room was filled with light. There were no barriers between things. Everything was energy, everything was light. Everything was interpenetrating with everything else. I looked across the bed and Justin was weeping, the tears pouring down his face. His face was luminous, like he had seen the face of God.

"The room is filled with light," he whispered. "Can you see it?"

"Yes," I replied.

"It's Grandma's last gift," he said. "She's holding open the door to eternity so we can have a glimpse."

He looked at me with such tenderness, and said, "You must feel so grateful to her." I realized then he had had a vision, too, and that I *was* grateful. He said, "You know, she was a very great soul. She had tremendous wisdom. She came and took a role much smaller than the wisdom she had, in order to give you something to resist so you could become who you are. Isn't there a word for that?"

The word he was looking for was Bodhisattva, from the Buddhist tradition. I think we are all Bodhisattvas in a way, in that we don't come for ourselves alone. We come because we grow as a group. We grow through what we share with other people. We grow through difficulties, perhaps more than we grow through the times when things go well. We are part of a greater holy and sacred mystery.

Here is the most important thing for you to keep in mind: you are never alone. If you could see, there are more beings of light here sustaining you than there are people in flesh bodies. You are never alone. Any attempt you make to become quiet inside, to pray, to bring forth a light for yourself makes a difference in this universe. As each one of us heals, we never heal alone. Our own healing always uplifts the whole of which we are a part.

~ *Joan Borysenko, Ph.D*

To See My Skye Again

There is no death! What seems so is transition;
This life of mortal breath
Is but a suburb of the life elysian,
Whose portal we call Death.
~ Henry Wadsworth Longfellow

After my beautiful eight-year-old daughter, Skye, died of Leukemia in 1968, I felt such a great loss. In Skye's short time with me, we had traveled the world together, lived in Australia and New Zealand, and on our last trip traveled on board a cruise liner to Egypt where we had an incredible time.

She and I were both highly intuitive and had the ability to see beings from other planes who walk on earth, so we shared something most mothers and daughters don't. We were very close.

We'd moved back to England two years before the tragedy. Shortly afterward, Skye developed flu like symptoms which turned out to be Leukemia. After my sweet Skye died, when I did sleep, I had a recurring dream in which I would be standing before a very large grey, early Georgian style house. Entering the house, I was always confronted by the same endless white corridors. In each dream the scene was replayed with me searching in absolute desperation to find Skye.

Occasionally I would meet what looked like a nurse or a doctor and would ask where Skye was. I would be pointed down one way or another and off I would go driven by the urgency of Skye needing me and knowing she was alone in her illness.

This terrible and haunting dream persisted for many months until one night it took a different turn. This time I entered the house as usual and followed the many corridors – where I was finally directed to go upstairs. I had never been upstairs before, and didn't know there was an upstairs.

There I found myself in what appeared to be a very large old-fashioned theatre sitting up in the gallery overlooking an immense stage. In the dim light I saw a line of children on the stage, singing. My eyes moved down the line and then I saw her. It was Skye on the end of the line, wearing her favorite sweater! Our eyes met in a moment of recognition. The love between us acted as a magnet, lifting both of us up and drawing us together. We exploded together in warmth and joy in mid air!

A feeling of wonderful warmth and delight surrounded me as I awoke. I had finally found my beloved daughter!

Many dreams followed where Skye would show up in shops, on streets or on buses. Skye always took my hand assuring me she was well and happy.

My Grandmother passed away in 1989. She and I had had a very close relationship. I had lived with her on and off in the war years. She had been like a second mother to me. When I was back in England in 1988 she told me she really wanted to die. She was 93 and many friends and most family were gone. She was frail and tired easily.

She wasn't afraid to die, and was quite psychic so we chatted about it, and I said to her, "Grandma, if you die please try and reach me if you can. Let me know how you are."

A few weeks after she died, Grandma appeared to me in a dream.

Her appearance was now of a 45 year old with hair curly and bobbed and she was dressed all in purple, with a long string of purple beads. The bizarre part was that she was riding an immense motorbike that looked like a Norton – and she was laughing and telling me it was wonderful. The dream was very real and I awoke from it feeling happy and jubilant.

I had the same dream some nights later – Grandma riding into my bedroom on this immense motorbike, dressed in purple, looking younger – and saying to me, "Look who I found."

Sitting perched behind her, blonde hair blowing as if in wind, was Skye. They were both laughing and happy and drove off through the wall.

I haven't had many dreams of them since that night. My dream was a true gift from heaven that has helped to heal the pain of their loss. Since then I've remarried and had another beautiful daughter that I named Skye. There are remarkable similarities between her and my Skye of those many years back. I always knew I'd see Skye again. I know that life continues and that real healing comes through knowing our loved ones live on even beyond this life.

~ *Patricia Orwin*

Ryan's Hope

... Weeping may remain for a night,
   but rejoicing comes in the morning.
                    – Psalm 30:5

The day started out normally enough. It was May 1, 1997. Ryan was upstairs preparing to leave for school, while his six-year-old sister, Jamie, waited for him at the front door. Suddenly Ryan started to tell us about Albert Einstein with such enthusiasm and excitement, it was as if a light had gone on in his head. He said, "E=mc2 – I understand what Einstein was saying: the theory of relativity. I understand now!"

I said, "That's wonderful," but thought, How odd. It wasn't his thinking about Einstein – Ryan was so intelligent – but rather the timing that seemed peculiar.

At ten years old, Ryan loved knowledge and seemed to have an abundance of it, far beyond his years. The possibilities of the universe were boundless to him. When he was in first grade, the children in his class were asked to draw a picture and answer the question, 'If you could be anyone, who would you be?' Ryan wrote: "If I could be anyone, I'd want to be God." At age seven, while sitting in church one day, he wrote:

The tree of Life, O, the tree of Glory,

The tree of God of the World, O, the tree of me.

Somehow I think Ryan just "got it."

In the midst of his strange outburst about Einstein, Ryan suddenly called out that he had a headache. I went upstairs and found him lying on his bed. He looked at me and said, "Oh, Mommy, my head hurts so bad. I don't know what's happening to me. You've got to get me to the hospital."

By the time we arrived at the hospital in Newmarket he was unconscious. We stood by helplessly as the doctors fought to save his life, and then they transferred him by ambulance to Toronto's Hospital for Sick Children.

A couple of hours later we were finally allowed to see him. He was hooked up to a life support system. When the doctor told us our son had suffered a massive cerebral hemorrhage and was "legally and clinically brain dead," it felt like a terrible nightmare. We went into shock. Nothing more could be done, the doctor said, and asked if we would consider organ donation. Astonishingly, we had discussed this with Ryan only recently. We looked at each other and simultaneously replied, "Oh yes, Ryan would have wanted that."

In April, Ryan had seen his dad filling out the organ donor card on the back of his driver's license. His dad had explained to him about organ donation and how you could help save another's life by agreeing to donate your organs when you die. When Ryan wondered if you needed a driver's license to do this, his dad replied that anyone could donate their organs.

Organ donation made such perfect sense to Ryan, he went on his own campaign persuading the entire family to sign donor cards. We had no doubt that donating Ryan's organs was the right thing to do.

After a small bedside service, we said our good-byes to our son.

When we left the hospital, we left a part of ourselves behind. Driving home, I could feel a thick fog roll in and surround me, crushing me. We were in total disbelief. My husband Dale, and I cried in each other's arms all that night and for many nights after. It was as if part of me had died with my son.

Grief consumed me for a long time. We kept waiting for Ryan to walk in the door. We grieved for the loss of today, and also for the loss of our hopes and dreams. I realize now you never get over the death of your child. With time you heal, but you are forever changed. It was our daughter Jamie who gave us a reason to get up in the morning and carry on.

Then on a beautiful morning four months after Ryan's death, the first letter arrived, addressed to my husband and me. As we read it, we both began to weep. It was from a twenty-year-old university student thanking us for our "gift of sight." He had received one of Ryan's corneas and could now see again. It is difficult to describe our emotions – we wept, but at the same time, we felt wonderful.

Sometime later, we received a second letter from a young woman of thirty who had received one of Ryan's kidneys and his pancreas. She'd had diabetes since she was five, spending much time in her recent years hooked up to a dialysis machine. She told us that because of Ryan, she was now free from insulin and dialysis, able to work again and return to normal life.

Early May brought the painful first anniversary of our son's death. Then we received our third letter. A young boy of sixteen, born with cystic fibrosis, had received Ryan's lungs. Without the double lung transplant he received, he would have died. Besides being able to return to school, he was now doing things he had never done before – running, playing hockey and roller blading with his friends. Knowing this boy's life had been renewed lifted our spirits immensely.

Due to confidentiality laws, organ donation is completely anonymous in Canada. However, organ recipients and their donor families can communicate through the organ transplant organization. Although we did not know the identities of the individuals who had received Ryan's organs, we were given updates about their health.

We learned about a six-year-old girl who had received Ryan's other kidney and was now healthy, free from dialysis and attending school full time. We also learned that the forty-two-year-old woman who had received Ryan's liver was doing well and was able to again spend time with her young family.

Such joy seemed to come from our sorrow, so much happiness from our loss.

Although nothing could take away our pain, we took great comfort and peace in knowing that Ryan had done something most of us will never do – he had saved lives!

That summer while on vacation in Haliburton, we met a young man – by sheer coincidence – who had had a kidney and pancreas transplant at the same hospital where some of Ryan's organs had been transplanted. He knew the young woman who had received her kidney and pancreas on May 2 from a ten-year-old boy he believed to be our son. Her name was Lisa, and she was doing great. Afraid to ask her last name, I later wondered if I might have passed on my only chance to meet one of Ryan's organ recipients.

This chance meeting inspired me, and the following spring I decided to share our experience with others. I'm not a writer, so it was a challenge to write our story and send it to the newspapers for National Organ Donor Week. I faxed my article to three papers, and to my astonishment, all three wanted to feature it! A flurry of interviews and photo sessions followed, and we experienced an excitement we thought we were no longer capable of.

When the first article appeared, Dale and I were totally overwhelmed when we opened the paper to find that Ryan's story of hope was the banner story – right on the front page! Included in the article was the poem Ryan had written when he was seven, just as we had it inscribed on his tombstone. We wept tears of joy and sadness as we read it over and over. In his brief ten years on this earth, our son Ryan had made a difference.

A few days later, the article appeared in the other two papers, and for a few weeks we received calls from people all across Canada. Surprised but delighted, we hoped the story would help raise awareness about organ donation and perhaps inspire others to donate.

Apparently Lisa also read the article. When she saw Ryan's poem, she recognized it from a letter we sent her and realized he was her organ donor. The article said we would be at the Gift of Life medal presentation in Toronto two weeks later, so she decided to attend. Once there, she was unsure about introducing herself. We all wore name tags, and when Lisa found herself standing next to my husband Dale she couldn't hold back. You can imagine the emotional scene of hugs and tears that followed! It was truly a miraculous, unforgettable moment! It felt so wonderful to see her standing there alive and healthy, knowing that our son had helped make that possible. Ryan's kidney and pancreas had apparently been a perfect match. A part of him now lives on in her.

Moments later, a woman approached us with her eight-year-old daughter. "I think my daughter has your son's kidney," she said. Kasia was just four when both her kidneys had shut down and she had gone on dialysis. The details of her transplant matched, and we all felt certain it must have been Ryan's kidney that had given this lovely girl a new life. A few weeks later when we visited Ryan's grave, we wept tears of joy when we found a beautiful drawing left there, signed "Kasia."

Due to Canadian confidentiality laws, meetings such as these are very rare, and it is impossible to describe the intense emotions that result. When Ryan died I thought I would never feel joy again. But meeting Lisa and Kasia was a kind of miracle, opening my heart to those feelings I thought had been forever buried with my son.

Today, I now know I will always be the mother of two children. Ryan is, and always will be, part of our lives. Although, the pain of losing him will never completely leave me, I have begun putting the pieces of my life back together, though it now takes a different shape. Part of our healing came from our experience of donating Ryan's organs. I am so grateful that God allowed me to meet Lisa and Kasia so my heart and soul could reopen. Meeting them allowed me to experience that "once in a lifetime" kind of feeling again, the one I thought was gone forever.

~ *Nancy Lee Doige*

If I Can Stop One Heart From Breaking

If I can stop one heart from breaking,
I shall not live in vain;
If I can ease one life the aching,
Or cool one pain,
Or help one fainting robin
Unto his nest again,
I shall not live in vain.

~ Emily Dickinson

My Mother and the Tree

We are the leaves of one branch,
the drops of one sea, the flowers of one garden.
~ Jean Baptiste Henry Lacordaire

My mother was an attractive woman in her youth. Her face was round, like a circle or moon. Thick dark hair. Sharp green eyes. She was average height but had an air of tallness. Fair Scottish skin, deep, dark red lipstick. There were shiny tubes of it on every windowsill in the house. The deep dark red matched the very deep dark passion in her heart. Her passion for nature, the elements, the spirit world.

When I was a child she taught me survival skills. If I were ever lost in the woods, "Make loud sounds and someone will hear you," she said. "Or follow a river downstream. Someone always lived at the end of a river."

My memories of childhood and holidays extend back almost to infancy. The traditional intertwined with the wonder of nature. The nature she was so conscious of. Shamrocks, and making the ice cubes in the refrigerator a light subtle green, like the shamrock itself. Cardboard Valentine hearts in the hallway and heart shaped cookies filled with strawberry preserves that she made herself from the back-yard berries. In the autumn there were bouquets of bronze and rust maple leaves in a tall livingroom vase. She peeled paper-thin slices of orange peels, then placed them on a low heated burner on the stove and the downstairs filled with the sweet scent of citrus. There were Easter baskets filled with straw from a farm a few miles away, jelly beans, real daffodils and a single standing bunny in cellophane. The constant combination of nature with our regular life. My mother took every opportunity to show us the closeness of nature. Our connectedness to it. Our oneness with it.

On the morning of Pancake Tuesday, the morning before Ash Wednesday, she wrapped nickels and pennies in wax paper, then dropped them deep into pancake batter. Every year we were treated to a feast of pancakes with maple syrup and little packages of coins inside the batter. The morning sun seemed to pour through the windows. As if the sky itself was bursting with joy. Its golden light pouring upon us like golden syrup. We ate the meal quickly and carefully, wanting to avoid the possibility of choking on nickels but also wanting to get to the next pancake and its possibility of currency.

My mother knew everything there was to know about gardening. She knew how to make any plant grow, anywhere. She transplanted things from the house into the woods and transplanted things from the woods into the house. She rooted things in water. She grew plants in the garden and in tin cans on window sills. Cans that once held stewed tomatoes were covered in wax paper and ribbons and housed scarlet geraniums. In her heart, she wanted to be one with nature. To be united with the storms, the moon, the stars and flowers and all of God's growing trees.

One of the last times I saw my mother she was eighty-three years old and alone in a Toronto hospital room, an IV hooked to her hand. Two small stuffed animals slept on her stomach. She looked like a very tall child who was simply trying to sleep.

She didn't remember me, but I told her who I was. I opened the miniature peppermint chocolates I'd picked up on the way and put one in her hand. She lifted it to her lips, then dropped it. It was too heavy. She looked up at me and our eyes shared a million memories in that one silent moment. Her eyes were hallways and I wandered through them to all the places I'd ever lived as a child, a young girl, and as a young woman who later became a mother herself. I saw her face everywhere. Her handprint was stamped on my sky. Her handprint was stamped on every aspect of my life. She was my mother, lover of nature, and she was leaving me.

We talked about the images she had in her mind. The clothes she saw me wearing. She said my shorts looked good. I was wearing a winter coat and a heavy wool scarf. In an almost inaudible voice she said that Pat was waiting for her out in the hallway. Pat, her sister, had passed away from breast cancer five years earlier. She whispered that Pat was there, outside the door, in the hallway, every day. She said that Pat was waiting for her. Pat would be the perfect person to help her cross over to the other side. I believe we all have someone who will help us cross over. An angel guiding us across the bridge.

I returned to the hospital room the following morning. My father sat in a hospital chair in the only corner of the room in shadows. He'd stayed beside her for weeks, his vigilance his final gift.

The nurse whispered to me, *"If you touch her hand and call her name she may open her eyes. But she's exhausted."*

I repeated *"Hi Mom ....,"* many times. *"Can you say Hi?"*

She opened her eyes, barely, and spoke in the same almost inaudible voice.

"Hhhhhhhhhhhiiiiiiiiiiiiiiiiiiiii............," as if now that she'd started the word she was completely incapable of ending it. *"Hi,"* was her final word.

We stayed for a while, my father and I, in silence, waiting for her soul to rest, for her spirit to soar to its next journey. Then somehow, on some level, we knew when it was time to leave. No one tells you these things in school or in adult life. It's something you know instinctively. When it's ok to leave the bedside.

My father was the last one to leave. I turned back to make sure he was ok. He was reaching for the bed lamp above her. Its harsh glare made her pale skin appear even whiter, bone white. His clothes were wrinkled from sitting for days, and his eyes, which I could finally see clearly, were swollen from tears.

With a motion I'd never seen before, he pulled the chain on the overhead lamp as if he were closing a large delicate book. He was allowing his partner of over half a century to rest. In peace. He pulled the silver chain and the room plunged into darkness. The only light from a moon shining outside the hospital window. Brilliant blue moonlight from nature wrapped itself around the room and around my mother.

I left Toronto a week later and returned to New York City and my view from the apartment window. I thought about the view of my neighbor's tree. The old Rousseau-like tree grew in a neighbor's courtyard next to my apartment, against a wire fence separating the courtyard from the rest of us in the neighborhood. Four thick branches extended up and out across entire buildings. The tree was probably 70 or 80 years old. Late at night, when things were quiet, wind rushed through the branches and made whooshing sounds, like surf, and I could imagine an ocean outside somewhere in the concrete city. People in the courtyard sat beneath its branches at candlelit tables, and the clink of their dishes blended with the sound of leaves in a breeze. Full moons appeared through the branches, and evening stars, storm clouds, lights from planes. In the morning, voices of schoolchildren echoed through the leaves. Green wooden benches and beds of manicured flowers bordered the tree on all sides.

Some trees live inside maintained gardens; others stand outside, withering on sidewalks. Some live a life of Russian roulette. I wrote about the tree and photographed it for over twenty years. It was an autumn blaze of topaz; December snow rested on its branches like hankies; in spring and summer it was alive with cardinals, blue jays, finches, and sparrows; pigeons rested like old people in rockers. Its branches stretched like mammoth arms, an unconditional friend at the end of unforgiving days, community in the best sense of the word.

But this week, following my mother's death, I returned to New York, paid the animated cab driver, carried my bag and my mother's ashes up four flights of stairs, put water on for tea, walked to the window, and looked through the glass to utter and complete emptiness. The tree had been chopped down while I was in Toronto. A fresh, sawed-off stump stood in its place. Everything else in the courtyard was intact. I yelled, *why* to no one. It was the middle of the night and there was no one to ask.

In the morning the man who looked after the garden was checking something in a flower bed near where the tree once stood.

"Can you hear me?" I called down.

"Yes," he said.

"Why was the tree chopped down?" I asked.

"Because six weeks out of every summer it drops things and no one can sit here," he said.

I was too heartbroken to ask why they couldn't sit somewhere else; the courtyard was the size of an apartment building. As we spoke, a bird flew in a path toward where the tree once stood, then stopped short and landed on a hedge adjoining the fence. There was already an emptiness, an unwanted silence and a very clear view of buildings and cement.

There's a theory that plants have an ability to communicate with one another, and possibly, with sufficient equipment, may in time communicate with humans. Plants may one day testify at a trial. That they respond to care and tenderness is a proven fact. Possibly the old tree and my mother had communicated during the past month. Both of them seeing into their future.

My mother who was so keenly aware of trees and earth will be associated in my mind with the tree, forever. They disappeared simultaneously. Two elderly souls deciding to travel together. Both of them knowing one another through me. Both of them teaching me about the sacredness and magic of this earth.

We can learn a lot from a mother. We can learn a lot from trees.

~ Magie Dominic

A Glimpse of My Mother's Soul

My father passed away in the winter of 2003. My 21-year-old daughter and I were with him at OSU (Ohio State University) medical center (my alma mater) and it was a peaceful, grace-filled experience that we will never forget.

Earlier that same week, I had placed my mother in an eldercare center because she could not be left alone. She has Alzheimer's/dementia and my father had been her primary caregiver. My father needed my immediate attention in the hospital and I saw no other option.

Before we took her to the center, she required a physical exam. As my daughters and I sat in the examination room with her, listening to the doctor ask her routine questions to determine mental competency, we noticed that she could answer very few. However, when he asked her to write a simple sentence the result was one that will stay with me and my three daughters forever.

When she finished writing, the doctor looked at the paper and said, "That's a wonderful sentence, Rose," and handed the paper to me. It read, 'LOVE CONQUERS ALL.'

I knew instantly that my mother had given me a gift, perhaps the greatest gift that she had ever given me – a glimpse of her soul – and a message, a profound affirmation that LOVE really is the greatest gift we can ever give each other.

I immediately left the room and sat outside in the parking lot to collect my emotions. Though it was the most difficult day of my life, putting my mother in a nursing home, I somehow knew that she understood.

~ *Carol Matthews O'Connor*

4

Healing to Move Ahead

This being human is a guest house.
Every morning a new arrival.
A joy, a depression, a meanness,
some momentary awareness comes
as an unexpected visitor.
Welcome and entertain all!
Even if they're a crowd of sorrows,
who violently sweep your house
empty of its furniture,
still, treat each guest honorably.
He may be clearing you out
for some new delight.
The dark thought, the shame, the malice,
meet them at the door laughing,
and invite them in.
Be grateful for whomever comes,
because each has been sent
as a guide from beyond.

~ Jalal ad-Din Rumi

THE HUG

We need 4 hugs a day for survival.
We need 8 hugs a day for maintenance.
We need 12 hugs a day for growth.
~ Virginia Satir

I always knew that I was different. First of all, it was the hair. My hair was very blond, almost white. My parents both had very dark hair. And then there was the face. I didn't look like either one of them. Then there was the fact that I was alone. As I looked around at other families, there were always several children with their parents. So right from an early age, I knew that I must be from some strange place, like Venus, and just here for a short sojourn. But the real concern about who I really was didn't start until I was five years old and started school.

For four years, I had been at home with my mother. I had no siblings so we were alone together during the day. Then that fateful first day of school arrived when I discovered that I had to share and interact in a pleasing manner with others. I spent a lot of time in the "corner" where the teacher sent those pupils who were "bad". So, not only did I not seem to belong at home, but I didn't seem to belong in the school environment either. Back at home, my parents could not understand why I couldn't fit in. Wasn't it obvious to them? My hair was different, my face was different and I was all alone. I became quiet and retreated into an inner world where I had my inner world friends who loved me and talked to me, and I was normal.

The first year of school passed and it was now summer. It was a hot, sultry summer day when my father came to me and said that my mother could no longer look after me. He had to go to work every day, so we would have to go to live with my grandmother. What had happened? Why couldn't she look after me? Why did we have to go to a strange place? This news confirmed my worst fears. My mother didn't love me. And if she couldn't care for me and didn't love me, it was probably because I was so different and didn't really belong to them. I was definitely from another planet. Life as I knew it was over. I was five and I was very depressed. Where would I find love?

I withdrew from happiness. There was nothing that could be done. My mother had been diagnosed with aggressive Multiple Sclerosis and her life, as she had known it, ended. Confined to a wheelchair, and with deteriorating physical and mental capacity, she needed ongoing support and care. Her support team was me and my father. It was a daunting daily task to keep the home going and make sure that mother could manage. Things done with love are a pleasure but of course I knew that she didn't love me, so each day was heavy with a sense of duty and obligation, rather than love.

The months stretched into years and mother's health became increasingly worse with many months spent in hospital. Our home became a dismal place, where a crisis, requiring a call to 911, always lurked around the corner. The years dragged on and I needed to search for love. There certainly appeared to be no love at home.

And then, on Christmas Day, after a long spell in the hospital, my mother died. It was over and now there was certainly no hope of ever finding love at home.

I think it was the ever-present loneliness that pushed me to seek one relationship after another. When I was thirteen, a boy named Charles carried my books home from school and that was the beginning of my long, and not so illustrious, search for love. I always looked outward to see who might want to be my friend and who could give me the loving attention I so craved. I wasn't fussy and that proved to be a serious problem as the years went on.

But finally I met a very nice man and we spent a lot of time together. This was fulfilling and happy and we were married. His career in motor racing took us all over North America and it was an exciting time in my life. I met new people and traveled extensively.

After five years of marriage, I began to feel a gnawing emptiness growing within me. I recognized this feeling. It said to me that the love in my life couldn't be real. It was an inner voice that invalidated my worthiness to receive love and that voice drove me to search again for 'true love'. But something happened that changed everything.

One afternoon I lay down for a little nap after work. During the nap a rather loud, but kind voice, said to me, "Barb, God is Love". When I awoke, I knew that my life would never be the same again. If love is God and God is love, then my search for human love all this time has really been a search for God in my life. I asked inwardly for a spiritual guide, someone who knew how to find God. It was a short time after this dream, that I came across a teacher, called the *MAHANTA, who taught about love and our true nature as soul. This gave life a whole new meaning; my focus was now to find the spiritual purpose of my life.

One of the ways I was helped was through understanding of the meaning of events in my life. For all these years I'd held a belief that my mother hadn't loved me. It had caused me to hold a part of my heart from life and to feel somehow separate.

Recently I'd gone through many changes and the separation of my partner of many years. A deep and painful healing was taking place. Then one night in a dream, I met my mother in the inner worlds. We greeted each other and were immediately drawn together in a warm and loving hug. As we embraced, I felt her warmth and waves of love poured through me. The waves undulated between us and in that moment, years of isolation dropped away as a tremendous realization surged up from deep within my heart. She had always loved me! It was I who had pulled away from love and isolated myself from her. My mother's love had always been there, but I hadn't been able to accept it.

There has been a spiritual healing: a true healing of the soul. In accepting my mother's love in this experience, it opened my heart to receive more love from others and to be able to give love more freely to those in my life. This is my spiritual purpose. I am no longer from another planet. I am here and ready to love and serve life and to feel the presence of God in every breath. Thanks Mom!

~ *Barbara Allport*

*MAHANTA is the name for the Guide of those on the path of Eckankar

He Sendeth Sun,
He Sendeth Shower

He sendeth sun, he sendeth shower,
Alike they're needful for the flower:
And joys and tears alike are sent
To give the soul fit nourishment.
As comes to me or cloud or sun,
Father! Thy will, not mine be done
Oh, ne'er will I at life repine:
Enough that thou hast made it mine.
When falls the shadow cold of death
I yet will sing, with parting breath,
As comes to me or shade or sun,
Father! Thy will, not mine, be done!

~ Sarah Flower Adams

Once Upon a Birthday

When I was a little girl, growing up on the southern Manitoba prairies, I would sometimes hurry from our yard, dash up the path and bounce up onto the sidewalk, where I would steal a stroll along the walk, until someone appeared, then I would quietly return to the grassy curb or the gravel. Although not one person was ever unkind, the feeling came from within me – I don't belong to this place. And so when I accidentally discovered I was adopted, I wasn't surprised at all.

The Canadian prairies and its people were slow to embrace change so, when I was growing up, right or wrong, illegitimacy was still an ugly thing. People of my town, and my adoptive parents were wonderful to me. Keeping the secret from me about my origins was done with the very best of intentions.

As an adult I learned that I was the illegitimate child of my adoptive mother's niece – no big deal. It was not an unheard of story – my biological mother had been married, had four children, then lost her husband suddenly to a car accident. Afraid and alone, she soon found herself penniless and pregnant by a man who didn't want her or her brood of children. She made an honest attempt to keep me after my birth, but soon came to realize the impossibility of her situation, so she offered me to my adoptive parents to raise as their own.

So I changed everyone's life. Phyllis, my birth mother, and my half siblings were never mentioned. No family member ever committed the grievous sin of speaking her name in my presence. Not one cousin, aunt or in-law ever broke the wall of silence my parents built around me. I learned she was my mother at the age of seventeen, but it took until I was twenty-four to learn where she lived and obtain a phone number. When that day came, elated and reckless, I called her immediately.

We hit it off at once. She sounded kind and warm, and I was drawn to her voice on the telephone with a force I couldn't identify. We made plans to meet in Alberta, where she lived with her husband and where most of her six other children also lived. At the last moment, for many reasons, but chiefly because I lacked the courage to go through with it, I didn't go.

She was terribly hurt, and felt betrayed. She had confessed her past to her children, and I had let her down. I knew that I had destroyed perhaps my only opportunity to have a relationship with my blood family. We never spoke again.

Indifferent to my pain, the years flew by. I teetered between periods of putting the whole thing behind me, to zealous attempts to find my mother and my siblings, neither of which bore any fruit. After a while, it became more like a lie than the truth. From time to time I would torment my adoptive parents with questions about my biological family, but they battened down the hatches and pulled the shade of secrecy, just as they had always done.

Otherwise, life was good. I was married to a great guy. With two young children we were a happy, busy family with a farm only twenty-five miles from where I grew up. Our house was filled with laughter and love and I was contented.

Then, in the fall of 1994, everything began to unravel. I became ill.

Sicker than I had ever been in my life, I had constant, terrible pain in my abdomen. I was terrified, weak and nauseated. I lost weight, my hair began to fall out, I cried constantly and I was obsessed with my health. I became convinced beyond a doubt that I had cervical cancer, and that it was advanced to a stage beyond treatment. Fear and pain dominated my existence. I couldn't take care of my family, and for the first time in my life I was too frightened to see a doctor. I seldom left our home.

My poor husband was completely at a loss. When not pleading with me to see a doctor, he cared for the children most of the time. Inevitably, I hit bottom, and in mid- December I called my family doctor after hours, and weeping uncontrollably, told him of my condition. A thorough physical examination proved me to be absolutely healthy, but I was suffering from a nervous breakdown.

Christmas 1994 saw me on medication and receiving treatment from a psychologist I knew personally. Together she and I searched for the cause of my mysterious emotional problems, and settled on my adoption and separation from my biological mother as the probable culprit. We talked and talked and gradually my demons began to retreat.

By July 1995, as well as being a seasoned veteran of counseling, I was also completely back to myself. The circumstances of my birth no longer haunting me, I had discovered that I loved and needed my biological mother as much as I needed my adoptive parents, and that was okay. I decided that now was the time to find her again, this time I knew things would be different. But when I told my adoptive parents of my decision, I was stunned to hear that she had died the previous year. They were unsure of the circumstances, except that it was an illness, and I had not been told because of my emotional state at the time.

The news hung in the air for what seemed like an eternity, and slowly I began to realize that I already knew what had happened to her. She had died from cervical cancer. I contacted her sister, the person who had provided me with her phone number all those years before, and she confirmed my intuitions.

I was left alone again, with the ghostly presence of a woman I never knew, but knew intimately. Finally, I understood the source of my pain the year before. Tears fell down my face in recognition of the fact that as my mother lay dying, I had shared her pain and anguish. I had wrestled with her fears. We were together in her death, just as we had been in my birth, and I realized what a wonderful gift my birth mother had bestowed upon me.

December 2000, my biological sister found me through the Internet, after I had given up all hope of ever finding my siblings. Our reunion was amazing. I felt an immediate connection to my three brothers and three sisters. We rejoiced to have all of us together. Whatever grief there may have been left in my heart was healed. In my sister's words, "We are seven." A current that was the soul and spirit of our mother runs through us all, binding us together.

I have talked at great length with them all about our mother's life and death. I discovered through my siblings, a woman who was funny, full of mischief, loved animals, was generous and played hard at life. I learned that my mother did indeed die of cervical cancer for which she refused treatment and pain medication. She entered the hospital only a couple of days before her death, and according to her nurse, held onto life by a weak thread and strong determination until she finally passed away on the 29th of December, 1994, my 32nd birthday! Our lives are like the Psalm Ecclesiastes 3:1: 'To every thing there is a season, and a time to every purpose under the heaven.'

Today my husband and I have a fourteen-year-old daughter, a twelve-year-old son, and a seventeen-month-old daughter who is full of mischief and life, loves animals and plays hard at everything she does.

~ Debbie McMechan

The Blue Jay

"If you are a gardener and find me,"
said the little bunny,
"I will be a bird and fly away from you."
"If you become a bird and fly away from me,"
said his mother,
"I will be a tree that you come home to."
~ From "The Runaway Bunny" by Margaret Wise Brown

It was on a hazy summer afternoon while I sat alone on our deck that the blue jay first flew toward me from the next-door neighbours' big elm. He appeared, seemingly from nowhere, upon the very branch I studied as I gazed immersed in the tree's subtle floating movements and shifting shades of green. Straightening in my lawn chair, my eyes fastened on his blueness as he winged toward me and landed on the railing not three feet away. He hopped twice to position himself facing directly toward me. His eye to my eye, he lifted the tuft on the top of his head in a way that seemed like a greeting, and with a knowing as sure as I knew my own name, I said in a whisper of my heart, "Hello Garrett."

Garrett.

Garrett, who would have been six this summer. Garrett, who

came to us and stayed too short a time. Garrett, who was poked and prodded and operated on; Garrett who couldn't ever eat and who, when he looked at you, saw into your soul.

"It's called 'gastroschisis' (gastro-skee-sis)", the specialist reading the ultrasound in my fourth month, told us. "There is a hole in the baby's stomach and the large intestine is protruding through it. He'll need some surgery to correct this as soon as he is born. In eight of ten cases it goes quite well."

But it doesn't go well when, in the womb, the hole closes over cutting off all circulation to the protruding bowel. After the surgery, only ten percent of the normal amount of bowel remained. We were told this would be insufficient for Garrett to experience the normal process of eating, digestion and elimination. He would never feel the pleasure and satisfaction of a meal or a snack and would need to be nourished in a special way through a tube directly into his blood stream, a process that would be very hard on his liver over time and that would negatively impact his ability to grow. How could we believe it when the pediatric specialist, looking like a child himself, shattered us with the news that our beautiful firstborn had only a fair to poor chance of seeing his first birthday?

It was easy to deny when, within four months, Garrett was able to spend part of each day at home in his own nursery, and when we amazed the health care professionals by learning to administer his complicated protocol and care program, the key factors to keeping him safely nourished and growing, infection free. Garrett was blossoming in the loving care of everyone around him.

Our life was overflowing with lullabies and toys, storybooks and cuddles, visits to the hospital, procedures, meds and x-rays. He handled each procedure with a patience that broke our hearts and when the pain was too much, like when it took multiple attempts to find a new vein for the intravenous, he would cry until so worn out, even making the smallest noise was impossible. His little body limp, I would see in his eyes that he had flown away. Then, when it was all over and safe to return, he'd come back smiling. If Ben should walk into the room, he would practically jump out of the arms of whoever was holding him to go giggling into his Daddy's magical embrace.

Developmentally normal in every other way, Garrett surprised everyone as he grew out of his baby clothes size after size, raising hopes that he could prove the doctors wrong. Each challenge that arose was successfully battled. "His line is infected; he needs surgery to insert a new feeding tube into his chest. Increase this med; reduce that one." And we cheered each and every baby milestone. "Look, he can pick up his soother! See that, he can reach the bears on his musical mobile! Hey, don't steal Nanny's glasses!"

Strange, how on some level though, we refused to see the yellow evidence of the liver damage in his face and eyes.

Having Garrett home most of the time, made our little family seem almost normal. A pet budgie bird named Blue arrived, and Garrett loved to watch him hop around the cage as we laughed at baby and birdie chirping in a language, all their own.

Eventually his progress made him a good candidate for a transplant. We yearned for the sound of the beeper that would mean there was a donor and Garrett would receive a new stomach, bowel, liver and pancreas. However, medical advances resulting in low fatality rates for children meant a small pool of potential donors. This, and the fact that donor and recipient must be very close in size, made the odds painfully low. We were forced to think about the hard decision of a pair of grieving parents. Could they decide to donate their child's organs so that the life of another could continue?

And so the waiting began.

But it was not to be. In the middle of the night in early June, suffering from liver failure, he was airlifted from Kingston to Children's Hospital in London, Ontario. Now topping Canada's organ donor list, Garrett would be with the transplant team and ready to go if a donor surfaced in time. On the gurney in the hallway outside of the Kingston ICU as the ambulance attendants prepared to take him to the airport, he smiled weakly and played with the stethoscope dangling from his doctor's neck. We all started to laugh and cry; the sweet baby – so sick, but he just wanted to play with a toy, like any other child.

London was a blur: a blur of routine. Catch a few hours sleep and then sit beside his hospital bed where he lay sedated, surrounded by machines in the intensive care unit. Devastated because we couldn't hold him, we read all of his storybooks to him: our favourite, "The Runaway Bunny" by Margaret Wise Brown. It's the tale of the little bunny who wants to run away, but is met at every turn by his mother's love as she promises to become, one by one, each destination he plans. The bunny finally decides he might as well stay home and be her little bunny.

"Please stay home with us, our little bunny. Please…"

But it was only a few weeks before a serious infection rendered Garrett too sick to stay on the transplant list. He went downhill fast and just one month before his first birthday we knew it was time to let him go.

The church overflowed with family, friends, co-workers, doctors, nurses. The minister, who had married us and baptized Garrett, and whose congregation had shared the journey with our family from day one, presided. "The Runaway Bunny" was read and the connection was drawn between the mother bunny's constant and unrelenting love for her little bunny and the nature of God's love for each of us.

The tears come less often now, but the love lives on and our missing him never fades.

God was wise when he sent Jack to us just over a year later, long and lean and blonde, bearing no resemblance at all to his rounder, darker, angel-brother. Wiser again He was to know we were ready when Logan popped out looking almost identical to Garrett – a resemblance we were ready to celebrate: a resemblance that grows less apparent now that Logan is nearly two and is taking on a look that is uniquely his own.

The blue jay's first appearance on the deck was about three years after Garrett's death when I was plump with Logan. Ben was at work and Jack napped safely in his first "big-boy" bed in the room he would share with the new brother (he knew his older brother, Garrett, had his own big-boy bed in Heaven, a place in the sky that he couldn't really see).

My heart lurched that first day when the Garrett-bird flew to me from the tree, like the bunny-bird in the story had flown to his waiting mother-tree. I didn't speak aloud for fear of making him fly away, but my heart said. "Hello, I'm glad you see us. I'm glad you're near." And so he hopped around me on the deck, like Blue, the budgie had in his cage, but like no other bird in the backyard had ever done before.

It seems Jack and Logan have their own special visits too. One day when I was scolding Jack for dangling off the side of Logan's crib, Jack came back with, "Why can't I, Mommy? Garrett does it all the time!" Immediately distracted, he ran off to the toy room before I had a chance to ask a single question.

The jay doesn't always show up, but sometimes when I'm alone out there he swoops in from one of the trees, and if he does I sit very still, my heart swelling while he hops close to me again, that crazy tuft waving. It makes me remember a chubby baby hand reaching for a dangling stethoscope and how very much I love him.

~ Judy Prang

as told to her by her daughter, Colleen Yeates.

A Pact Made in Heaven

We never know how high we are
Till we are called to rise;
And then, if we are true to plan,
Our statures touch the skies.
~ Emily Dickinson

I was in shock and disbelief as I looked at the picture I'd found in an envelope from my mother's personal effects. She and I had been very close and shared just about everything, so discovering she'd kept secrets from me was hard to understand. She'd recently passed away from Cancer. I was charged with having to go through her personal effects when I came across the envelope containing documents that revealed my mother had given up a baby girl for adoption. I was shaken as I looked over pictures of my much younger mother holding a tiny baby. How could this be?

How could my mother, my best friend, keep this a secret all these years?

When I called my father for answers he revealed that my sister was several years older than me and that she was my "full" sister. When the baby arrived, my parents were simply too young to care for an infant. My mother named her baby Sandra Lee. I realized it must have been devastating for my mother to give up her precious infant because when I was born eight years later she named me Sandra Leigh as well.

I was convinced that my mother left this information for me to find. What was too painful in life would be shared in death. My father told me he hadn't known the letter or the pictures existed. I decided right then and there that I was going to find my sister if it was the last thing I did and set about over the next few weeks gathering the paperwork. I needed to begin my search.

Exactly three months later after waiting on pins and needles I received the exciting call telling me they had located my sister. I was elated with the news! And best of all, she was only a few hours away and willing to have some contact with me. I immediately wrote a letter to my sister explaining who I was and filling her in on other details I had.

Two weeks later, I was in my car when my cell phone rang. I nearly drove off the road when the voice on the other end said, "Hi Sandra…it's your sister calling." The tears streamed down my face as we spoke for about twenty minutes, trying to fill in the empty spaces and the question marks. From that day forward we began to form our friendship and three months later we decided to meet face to face. I can't recall ever being as emotional.

As I approached the little town of Dashwood, and pulled into the driveway of my sister's home, I realized that our meeting would change the rest of my life.

I walked into the house and before I got to where she was standing, I was crying uncontrollably. Here was the spitting image of my mother standing in front of me! We spent the next twelve hours talking, eating, laughing and sharing. It was the most amazing day of my life.

During that afternoon we discovered that our mothers, mine who had given birth to both of us and hers who had raised her, shared some amazing similarities. Both had a joy for life, an infectious laugh and a twinkle in their eye. So many positive similarities and yet there were the negative ones too. My mother died from cancer and her mother was dying of cancer as we spoke. Here were two women who put the world on their shoulders and were selfless beyond belief. They would always lend an ear for someone else, but never ever shared their grief, their pain, their secrets, or their dreams, all of which took a toll I am sure. The summer came and went and my sister and I were getting closer and closer.

As each month went by I wished I could meet her mother. I wanted to know this wonderful person who'd adopted my sister. On Labor Day weekend my whole family came to Dashwood to meet my sister. To my delight, who walked up the driveway, but my sister's mother. What a brave soul she was to show up unannounced to meet her daughter's newfound family. It was a wonderful day. We talked and we laughed and when she was too tired she laid down for a nap. She decided to return home after dinner and we had a tearful goodbye. How was I to know that would be the first and last time I would ever see her?

Two weeks later I received a phone call from my sister that her mother was admitted to hospital and was failing fast. I gave her all the support I could, having just gone through this almost a year earlier. A few days later she succumbed to her illness; the same illness that stole my mother from me.

How could this happen? Is the world this cruel? Or was it perfect timing and fate? I lost my mother, but gained a sister I had wished for my whole life. She lost her mother, but gained a family she had been secretly yearning for her entire life. Sometimes I think this was planned long before we ever came to this lifetime. A plan devised from somewhere very far away.

Is it possible that two souls made a pact to come into this lifetime and share the upbringing of two little girls and when these girls needed each other the most, the opportunity would arise for them to meet? It may seem a little far-fetched, but somehow it's the only way to accept the loss of my mother. It's the only way to explain how two amazing women were taken from their families, long before it was time for them to go.

Sometimes I have this dream at night and in it I see two women standing side-by-side holding hands, looking down on two women standing side-by-side and saying to each other: "We did a good job didn't we!"

~ *Sandra Irvine*

Runway to Heaven

The greatest thing you'll ever learn
is just to love and be loved in return.
~ Eden Ahbez

I sat by her hospital bed holding my mother's gaze. Eyes that I knew so well looked back at me with love. A nurse bustled into the room, then fussed and tucked the soft crocheted afghan snugly around her.

My mom said, "Don't touch me. I am a star!"

The nurse shot me a conspiratorial look, saying, "Don't be alarmed, it's the medication."

I smiled, realizing mom was recalling her youth, when as a model she had been a star of the runway. Though her blue eyes were receding into her cheekbones and looked too large for her face, they remained alive and full of merriment. The end of her life was near but for a brief moment she still commanded the runway.

She drifted in and out of sleep, eyelids fluttering, a myriad of expressions flitting across her face. My mind drifted back to my earliest memories of the woman who gave me my life.

I recalled the trunk my mother kept, full of pictures of herself when she was a successful runway model in New York and Montreal. During the 1930's and 40's her beautiful face and body adorned the cover of dozens of magazines. During World War II she was the Canadian 'It Girl', modeling for fashion designers, catalogues and hundreds of advertisements.

As a little girl, I loved it when she pulled out the trunk of photographs and told me stories of her glory days. Then she'd walk around as if on the runway. "This is how I strutted my stuff," she'd say, while turning her heel in a way that guaranteed you would never lose your balance.

While she lost herself in the memory of applause, I looked at the pictures of the beautiful blonde, blue-eyed girl who was Veronica Lake, Carole Lombard and Bette Davis all rolled into one. Then in her theatrical style, she'd tell me the story of how she and my dad first met. "During the war at a Red Cross dance, I spotted a service man who took my breath away. I casually dropped my white opera glove near him. He stooped to pick it up. I swear it was love at first sight for both of us."

Then she'd hand me the photos of a glorious looking couple: dad so handsome in his Air Force uniform, and mom so beautiful. I remember wondering, "Did I have to be beautiful to be loved by her? Were her memories more important to her than I was?"

When the last of my two sisters was born, the career that defined her abruptly ended. The trunk that held the pictures and yellowed newspaper clippings remained in her room, but over the years was opened less and less. The years passed and mom became more and more reclusive. As these Agoraphobic tendencies developed, her fears of driving a car, riding on a bus, going on an airplane, or being in public places took over her life. Eventually, she rarely left the house. Instead, she wanted the world to come to her.

I remember being hurt when my school friends came to visit her more than me. Mom would transform back into her old vivacious self as we all gathered around her in the living room for modeling lessons. She loved being the centre of attention. There were often a dozen girls at a time in our house, all balancing books on their heads and practicing their runway walk while mom corrected and praised us.

"Keep your back straight and your head held high," she'd tell us. "And don't forget to focus straight ahead. Look life straight in the eye!" Mom knew what that meant. At only 5-foot 4-inches, her short stature never stopped her from going after her dream of becoming a model.

While mom isolated herself in her room for days at a time, Dad, a salesman, traveled for two weeks each month, leaving me to raise my two younger sisters by myself. I felt my mother had abandoned me and I didn't know why. Over the next twenty years, I watched her slip further and further away and there was nothing I could do.

As I grew into a young woman and moved away from home, her jealousy took control and she would lash out with hurtful words like, "You're ugly!" In time I came to understand that she was just voicing her own fears about the fact she was aging. It was sad to see her inspecting each and every wrinkle in front of her lighted vanity mirror.

Then a miracle happened. At seventy years old, her only granddaughter was born to my middle sister. Love for this baby girl gave mom the courage to leave the house, giving her a new lease on life. She was finally out in the world again, even if she hid behind big sunglasses and scarves like an aging movie star. We all benefited from her newfound "youth." Emotionally she had conquered the Agoraphobia, taking us on shopping sprees, out to movies and dinner. Her life was finally back on track. Unfortunately this period was all too brief, for in my niece's fifth year, mom's heart began to give out. It broke her heart that she could no longer pick-up her beloved granddaughter.

As the months passed, mom's heart grew steadily weaker. During this time my sisters and I were constantly by mother's bedside. As her primary caregivers, with full time jobs as well, it was a stressful time. My youngest sister eventually moved in to relieve some of the pressure.

Even though Mom had had such a great fear of death and aging, during her illness she demonstrated great maturity and strength. She now focused her attention on her three beautiful and beloved daughters. We spent her final days gathered around her, giving her nothing but unconditional love.

Even in ill health she had words of wisdom for us and said many times, "Don't be afraid to be who you are. I gave you your wings. Spread them wide!"

On October 16, 1993 my middle sister reported that she sat bolt upright from her sleep with a deep gasp, feeling like it was mom's last breath. Later that evening, at around midnight, I was writing in my journal, when I saw a radiant light appear at the foot of my bed. There was mom, young, beautiful, and shimmering.

She said, "Always remember to love yourself. You are beautiful just the way you are." Tears welled up in my eyes for I knew it was her way of apologizing. I forgave her, telling her how much I loved her, and then she went into the light and slowly faded. Moments later my youngest sister reported seeing mom walking out our driveway and into the distance, headed for the runway to heaven.

Mom was my greatest teacher. Today whenever I doubt myself, I remember her words, "Always remember to love yourself." Mom taught me that no matter what we may achieve in life, the only lasting thing is love.

~ *Marilyn J. Milne*

Memories of a Special Soul

The love you withhold is the pain you carry.
~ The Andromedans

My husband and I had just returned from seeing the movie RENT. It is an amazing depiction of a play that ran on Broadway for over 10 years. It is a poignant story about a special group of people who are on the verge of being homeless. Most of them are HIV positive.

The lead singer reminded me so much of my son who passed away from AIDS, that at one point in the movie when the lead is attending a support group, I began to sob. For the rest of the movie I couldn't stop wiping my eyes as I remembered my son Jeff, and grieved through those terrible feelings of sorrow.

I will never forget the first time I saw him; he was riding on the hip of a nurse and just quietly looking around. The baby daughter of my roommate was wailing away, as she bounced on the nurse's other hip.

When the nurse put Jeffery in my arms, I felt as though I was in the presence of a special being, a very wise old man who was sizing me up. Little did I know what an incredible journey was about to begin for the two us.

When Jeff was just a newborn, my neighbor and I used to go to the beach every morning in Florida before the sun became too hot. I would place Jeff on a pad with an umbrella over his little body. At only 3 weeks old he already had a marvelous tan from the reflection of the sand and water. We would stop on the way home to have a bear claw and fresh squeezed orange juice. Jeffery would sit on my lap making sounds, "uh-uh-uh". Finally I figured out that he wanted a drink. He'd gulp down the orange juice just as though he had been doing it for years, and the people in the restaurant would marvel at this tiny baby who, unlike any other, could drink from a glass. It was so much fun.

Everywhere we went, whether it was the grocery store or a restaurant, he attracted crowds of people. I would think of the stories that were told about Jesus and I would wonder, "Just who is this baby?" I had never seen anything like it before.

Always ahead of the game, his first teeth popped through when he was only two months old. It was like he was in a big hurry to get on with everything. He never crawled; at only seven and a half months, he just got up and walked. Later I learned this wasn't good news, because babies need to crawl as part of their brain development.

My first husband and I were convinced we had a genius on our hands, because at the age of 2 he was identifying cars by their make and pronouncing their names. I remember, as if it were yesterday, seeing him point and say, "Cadwak" and "Bolksvagen". He really was a very precocious child. His father was a car buyer and we thought for sure he would follow in those footsteps.

But, when we discovered our very smart little boy was having a terrible time in school, we were concerned. Then, one afternoon Jeffery revealed to me that he was seeing 2 glasses of juice and didn't know which one to pick up. The reasons for many of the puzzling things that were happening, such as Jeff spilling his milk or juice constantly, became very clear when we learned Jeffery was dyslexic. A specialist told me the awful truth: learning would always be difficult for Jeff, unless all teaching was done orally.

Since this was not possible, school remained a nightmare for him. Here he was, with practically a genius IQ, and he could barely read.

Jeff was just 15 when he made the move to Detroit to live with his father, from whom I'd been divorced for 12 years. Jeff was extremely excited about starting a new life. For awhile he seemed to do quite well in his new life, but the next year, at only 16, he quit school and fell in with a bad crowd.

I had no idea that it would be many years before we saw each other again.

One night, several years later, I had a dream in which I was at a party with a group of friends. There was a knock at the door. I opened it to find a stranger. He was invited in and proceeded to tell one of the mothers at the party that her daughter had translated (I knew this meant she had died). Everyone gathered around and tried to console her. Then the stranger turned to me and said, "Your son is also going to translate soon." At the time of that dream I had not seen my son for years. A few weeks later, I had another dream. In this one I looked out the window and saw a black motorcycle coming up the driveway, driven by a rider, all dressed in black. As I went to answer the door, the dream ended.

Two weeks later, I was looking out the window, and to my amazement, a black motorcycle came up the driveway. I went to answer the door, just like in the dream. At first I didn't recognize the person who was standing there. The last time I'd seen my son he had long blonde hair, a beard and mustache. Now Jeff was clean shaven and his hair was pulled back in a ponytail. My heart skipped a beat and exploded in joy.

He had come to ask for my help. He said he was ready to change his life and wanted to go into rehab. My husband and I were ready to do whatever it took to help him.

Within a few days he was admitted to a very well known rehab hospital. While there, Jeff learned he was HIV positive. He had suspected this for awhile and when he heard the news he was very calm and told me, "I know this is a gift from God. I am not afraid. I am grateful for a second chance to straighten out my life and get back on the right path." Words cannot express the gratitude I felt when I heard him say this. I felt like I had been waiting forever for this moment.

When his stay at rehab was over, we brought him home, where we could care for him and help him get well. My husband is a holistic physician, which means that he treats the whole person, not just the physical symptoms. He put Jeff on regimen for healing, including: vitamins, minerals, herbs, proper nutrition and lots of hugs. We did a great deal of research, and whenever we heard about a new method of treatment we incorporated it into his healing program. Over time, Jeff began to improve, and he continued to do well for about 2 years. It was a lovely and loving time and we were grateful to be together, enjoying every precious minute.

Nobody knows exactly what happened or why, but slowly Jeff's health began to deteriorate again. He became a paraplegic and was completely bedridden. All the while he never complained, nor bemoaned his fate.

We took care of him at home for about four months with the help of many others, including the families, parents and friends of other AIDS patients. Then finally, we couldn't do it anymore. I cannot express the gratitude I feel for those who helped us. As well, I gained strength through my beloved spiritual path, *Eckankar*, without which I don't think I could have survived the ordeal.

One very endearing memory I have of my son was his ability to give attention to everyone who came into contact with him every day. At the time I did not quite understand what he was doing, but later I realized that he was spreading Divine Love to everyone. It didn't matter to him if they were grumpy or even ignored him. Jeff had a knack of connecting to people and he always acknowledged everyone he met.

It absolutely broke our hearts when we had to place him in a nursing home.

The day he no longer recognized anyone, my wonderful husband thought that I needed a respite, so he made arrangements for a trip to New Orleans. The very first night we went out to dinner and returned to our room to see the red light blinking. With great trepidation we retrieved the message. Just as we both feared, it was a call from the nursing home telling us that Jeff would not live through the night. My sister was there and said to him, "Don't you dare die; your mother is coming. Wait for her."

We took the first plane out and arrived at his side about noon. He had indeed waited for us. Kissing him goodbye, we told him it was okay to go. We read to him from *"Stranger by the River"*, a book of prose describing a seeker's journey, then sang "HU," a love song to God that harmonizes one's surroundings and opens the heart to love. As we opened our eyes, Jeff took his last gentle breath, and was gone.

Thus, the journey of his life with us ended. We were so grateful that he had waited for us to come. It was a privilege to be with him one more time and to say goodbye.

Jeff was just twenty seven-years old.

His ashes are buried in the front yard. Because it was his favorite animal, we have placed a white concrete cat with incredible blue eyes near the spot. When I walk nearby, the cat's eyes, so like Jeff's own bright blue ones, seem to follow me. They remind me of how much I still love and miss him.

~ Jacquelyn Mantell

She Prayed for a Sign

Jeanette Wilson and I met through our sons in 1978. The boys were both six years old and blonde. That year it seemed like a thousand youngsters, ours included, wanted to play soccer. The boys were precious. It was not unusual for them to stop and pick a flower or get carried away watching butterflies. At their age they wanted to play, but they were also immensely interested in the world around them.

We moved away in 1984 and I didn't see Jeanette again for six or seven years. By then, my son had been killed in a car accident (age 17). Jeanette and I met again in Lethbridge. She had moved there and I was in the city preparing for my father's funeral. I do not believe our meeting was a coincidence. We renewed acquaintances and exchanged new addresses. When next I heard from her, and it was only months later, she had written to tell me that Brian, her son, was dead, killed in a motorcycle accident. I knew her pain. She knew mine. I tried to picture the reunion of these two blonde soccer players!

Brian had died close to home, in an ambulance, while his mom sat and prayed for him. She told me it had been a nice day and Brian and his brother had gone for a short motorcycle ride. They were so close to home when the accident happened. Close enough for Brian's parents to get to the scene to be there for him and to pray for him. Like so many ahead of her, Jeanette, following the death of her son, struggled with her faith in God, in her close relationships and in life itself. She fought through bouts of depression and tried to sort out who she was. In her words, "I feel there is a great loss of dignity when you lose a child."

It was close to two years after Brian's death that Jeanette asked God for a sign that her son was indeed with Him in Heaven.

Jeanette wrote, "Some time later at Easter service I received an answer. The choir was singing beautifully at the front of the church and, in my mind's eye, I could see Jesus standing and listening alongside them. He was holding Brian's hand and I could see Brian's face and features so clearly. He was smiling and just glowing with joy and peace. Since that time, when I picture Brian, that is what I see. Through the sadness of missing Brian, it helps me to accept his death more easily and I continue to thank God for this gift."

~ *Ellie Braun-Haley*

Becoming Conscious

Other people may be there to help us, teach us,
and guide us along our path.
But the lesson to be learned is always ours.
~ Melody Beattie

As I stood at the phone listening to the news from my husband that my mother had just had a heart attack, I was stunned. We'd been instructed to have no outside contact during the week of the workshop, so when I received a message that my husband had called in the first hour of the program, I was very perturbed.

The whole reason I'd come to the week long workshop in 1979 was to finally have healing on issues surrounding the volatile relationship with my mother. I'd finally found the courage to deal with what I perceived to be her dominance, her criticism, her rejection, her anger – all the behaviors that I believed had scarred my life – somehow she'd managed to find a way to interfere. How could she do this to me?

Sadness and fear overcame me and I sobbed uncontrollably on my bed. I felt completely unable to decide what to do. The course instructors let me know that I would have to make the choice. As I sat in my room wracked with pain, tranquility began to fill my room. I could feel my mother's presence as I sat there alone. Holding my breath, I felt her warmth and protection encompassing me. She said clearly, not so much in words but as an impression, 'Come home. You don't have to do this – it's too painful. Come home.'

I was shaken by the message and startled by how it had come to me. Then I realized that my mother was throwing me a lifeline. I was witnessing, first hand, how we can communicate on a spiritual level. My mother wanted to protect me from the pain that she knew I was about to face.

In my more composed state, I was able to call home for an update. As if somehow the divine hand of God had intervened in these events, I learned my mother was out of danger and would be okay.

I breathed deeply and decided to continue with the workshop. I silently thanked my mother and told her that I had to do this. It was an enormous turning point as I made the choice to do what was right for me. I decided in that moment that I would now live in a conscious way instead of hiding from feelings and thoughts.

When I saw my mother a week later, she had just been released from the hospital. As I entered the room, our eyes joined. In that communication, we met on new ground. Kneeling in front of her, we held each other. I will never forget the look in her eyes or the feeling when she held me so tenderly, as if I were her baby all over again. For the first time, we were giving each other love, honest and pure. Now I understood that she had done the best she could. I no longer need-ed to blame her for the past or the present. I knew that our relation-ship would never be the same.

This moment was important for it gave us strength for what was ahead.

Within two weeks my father, who was undergoing cancer treat-ments, was told that he had only a few weeks to live. Every day I spent time with him at the hospital doing what I could to make him comfortable. In the evenings, I stayed with my mother and heard her pour out the stories of their life together. Our time together was very special and I cherish those memories.

It would be a long journey, but both of my parents improved and live in the family home to this day. My father's recovery has been called a miracle. For me, the miracle occurred on the side of my bed in 1979 when I began my conscious journey.

~ *Daryl Wood*

A Gift of Love

If you would have love, you must first give love.
And if you give divine love to others, you shall have divine
love for yourself.
~ Harold Klemp, *Love the Keystone of Life*

Traveling in a train driven by a steam engine can seem both terrifying and exhilarating to a four year old child. It was 1945 and it was my first travel experience. My family was moving from my birthplace in Lower Largo, Fife, to the lovely village of Ballachulish in Argyll, Scotland. The mountains there are as high as the lochs are deep, and the warm-hearted natives strive to live in harmony with their surroundings.

Because my dad was a minister, our new home was the United Free Church Manse, which had recently been built in front of the old church. There was no electricity in that area of Scotland at that time, so we burned peat or coal in the fireplace for heat, and used paraffin lamps for light.

Behind the house and church flowed the Larach River, singing its way over large rocks and stones. Its daily song was an invitation to adventure and the mystery of what might be found on the other side. One day, curiosity overcame me, and without thinking I went against my dad's wishes and crossed the river. The only thing I remember about the other side is the distant image of my dad riding his bike home. In my hurry to jump from rock to rock before my dad saw me, I fell into the fast moving current. Fortunately my mom saw me from the kitchen window and hurried to pull me out of the icy water before my dad got home.

While sitting on our front lawn picking buttercups or making daisy chains, I would often drink in the beauty of the mountainside and gaze longingly at the local school which was situated across the road and behind the principal's house. It seemed to me that every child in the area went to school except my younger brother and me. Somehow, my fifth birthday seemed like an eternity away!

My patience declined as this longing for knowledge grew, until one day I found myself banging my fists on the door of Miss Cameron's classroom, insisting that I be allowed to join the school. I had to persist in this fashion for several days before Miss Cameron finally relented and allowed me to enter her sacred domain. Within a few weeks my joy turned to sorrow, as the whole class became ill with scarlet fever! Being an acute, febrile, contagious disease, there was a sudden mass exodus of children to the fever hospital a few miles from the village.

One night, my temperature spiked to 105, and I had to be transported by taxi to the country hospital. In addition to a red rash, the pain in my nose, throat and mouth was so severe that I was afraid to cry for fear of making my condition even more unbearable. Surely I must be dying! To make matters worse, I was also diagnosed with rheumatic fever. No visitors were allowed and so, once a week, my dad would ride into the hospital grounds on his bicycle, and I was allowed to wave to him from the window near my bed. He brought me gifts of "blood oranges" for my health, and those were shared with all the other children. Although the nurses were extremely busy, they were always very kind and compassionate.

Because of the rheumatic fever, I remained in hospital a lot longer than my classmates, and was given a considerable amount of tender loving care by the staff. As a result of this experience, I knew, at this young age, that someday I would definitely become a nurse.

In 1959 I was accepted by The Western Infirmary in Glasgow for nurse's training and eventually became a registered nurse. I then moved to my parent's home in Paisley for a while so that I could train as a midwife. When I immigrated to Canada in 1967, I worked as a delivery room nurse because midwifery had not been legalized there at that time. I cared for many wonderful patients over the years, but there is one patient who will always stand out from the rest because her gratitude, under very painful circumstances, touched the very core of my heart. To protect her identity, I will call her Jean.

I was working in the labor and delivery assessment room one day when Jean, accompanied by her mom, arrived to be assessed. I learned that Jean's baby was overdue and that she hadn't felt any baby movements at all that day. Because the baby's father was no longer in the picture, Jean's mom had accompanied her for support. When the fetal monitor failed to pick up the baby's heartbeat, her doctor was notified and an ultrasound ordered. The dreaded answer came when the ultrasound confirmed that the baby had indeed died.

My heart went out in sympathy to this young mother and grand-mother. I encouraged them to talk about their pain and feelings of loss, and listened to them with an open heart. Eventually it was decided that Jean would go home for the night and come back for induction of labor the next morning.

When I came into work early the next day, I asked specifically if I could be assigned to Jean, instead of working in the assessment room. Jean was pleased with this arrangement because of the bond of friendship that now existed between us. The induction of labor progressed well, and Jean was given an epidural so that her delivery would be a pain-free experience. When the delivery was imminent, her doctor was called in to deliver the baby. Jean delivered a beautiful, black-haired, stillborn baby girl.

When we saw the cord tightly around the baby's neck, we knew the reason for the baby's demise. I quickly washed the baby's face, while the placenta was being delivered, and wrapped her up in a pink blanket so her mom and grandmother could hold her. This was truly a most heartbreaking experience!

With a very sad heart, I cut a lock of dark hair for Jean to keep as a memento, along with a set of her baby's footprints. Jean wept as she held her baby for a long, long time before being transferred to a private room on the ward.

When I said goodbye to Jean that evening, I never dreamed that I would ever see her again. Two weeks later the delivery room doorbell rang, and over the intercom a woman asked to speak specifically to me. I opened the door, and to my great surprise Jean was standing there with a gift in her hand. Inside the box was a lovely Noritake fine china cup and saucer she had bought to thank me for all my care. Along with the cup was a copy of the beautiful poem she had composed for her daughter.

This was probably one of the most touching moments of my life, as I thought of all the hundreds of mothers I had cared for who take their babies' lives and health for granted. Despite her grief and pain, this lovely lady took the time to show me her gratitude. I had a hard time choking back the tears as I hugged her in thanks.

I have been retired from nursing for almost five years now, and on occasion, very early in the morning, you will find me sipping tea from a Noritake cup while thinking fond thoughts of Jean. I am pleased to say that Jean eventually married happily, and delivered a healthy baby girl.

~ *Sybil Barbour*

The Right Words

Listening is a magnetic and strange thing, a creative
force...When we are listened to, it creates us,
makes us unfold and expand. Ideas actually begin to grow
within us and come to life...When we listen to people there is
an alternating current, and this recharges us so that we
never get tired of each other...and it is this little creative
fountain inside us that begins to spring and cast up new
thoughts and unexpected laughter and wisdom.
...Well, it is when people really listen to us, with quiet fascinated attention that the little fountain begins to work again,
to accelerate in the most surprising way.
~ Brenda Ueland

"Stop mom, don't do it. There's a car beside us!"

I was about to change lanes on a busy highway when my son
called out the warning. Looking over my left shoulder, I saw that a
vehicle held the space I had intended to move into. My son constantly amazed me with his sense of timing, how he would always deliver
the right words, at just the right time.

I look back at one incident and smile. Jason had been bouncing
his soccer ball off the wall after a neighbor had complained it was
irritating. Despite my warning, he was back at it again! Infuriated, I

began shouting at him to stop. But Jason, a 6-foot 2-inch tall muscular athlete walked over, and with a huge smile just picked me up. It was futile. I tried to continue lecturing, but my anger had melted.

Another time, I'd been given a yellow, hooded sweatshirt by the staff at a Catholic Separate School as a thank you gift for teaching dance to their students. When Jason saw the sweatshirt, featuring the rival school's football team name and logo, he said, "I hope you're not planning on wearing that, mom!"

"Why not, it's new and nice looking." I responded.

A few days later, I arrived home to find Jason wearing the very same hoodie. Surprised, I asked, "Surely you didn't wear that to school today?"

"Yes," he replied, "I did."

"Oh my goodness," I said, "What happened?"

"Well," he answered calmly, "they threw me up against the lockers and called me names."

I said, "Oh Jason, I guess you won't be doing that again!"

"Why not, mom? It builds character!" he said.

That same spring of 1989, Jason was competing in the Western Canadian Track and Field competition. In the morning, he hugged me just before he left to drive to the event. All that day it felt as if everything were out of sync. It was just a wretched day. Later that evening when Jason hadn't returned home at the expected time, I phoned the police. They assured me there were no car accident reports, but I couldn't shake the feeling that something was wrong.

An hour or so later a policeman came to the door. I could tell by his face something was very wrong. No words can describe my horror when in the next instant he delivered the terrible message – my son was dead!

"No," I begged the officer. "He's really all right. He's just hurt. Take me to him. He's just hurt. Please tell me he's just hurt!"

Our hug early that morning was to be our last, for I learned shortly, that he'd lost control of his car, and within minutes, was dead.

I was in a state of numbness. My reality was shattered. There would be no more balls bouncing against the walls – no more late night gabfests, or shopping together late at night for groceries.

No more Jason.

I learned later from the people driving behind him, that his car suddenly veered out of control for no apparent reason. Our family doctor surmised that Jason must have suffered an aneurism. I never learned if it were true, for each time I tried filling in the request for the accident's medical report, I wound up sobbing uncontrollably.

For the next several months I felt that I was in a dream. I was overwhelmed with such immense sorrow that I couldn't speak. For a long while I didn't recognize people, and couldn't recall the names of friends I'd known for years.

I had no idea how I would go on. Then three months after Jason's death, I stood in church surrounded by hundreds of people, observing a mother and son who were in the crowd and feeling tortured at the realization I would never hold my son again. Suddenly Jason was standing beside me, on my left. I could even smell his aftershave.

"You haven't lost me mom. I'm still here," he said.

Time stood still. There was no other sound. No movement. There was just my beloved seventeen year old. I felt such comfort for the first time since his death. And then a realization struck. Death hadn't separated us. There still remained a tie between us.

The following day I decided to test this connection and said, "Jason. I can hardly wait until I die so we can be together again." Once again, I heard his voice so clearly, as though he was at a distance and had turned to speak to me. "You came to this earth with a plan," he said. "There are unfinished tasks you still need to complete." Then he told me to, "Live for today."

I knew then I needed to honor Jason. That meant living my life now, while cherishing the time we'd been given while he was here.

Something about my meeting with Jason must have started a divine agreement, because inexplicably, over the next few weeks, strangers began sharing their stories with me. They were true stories, like my own, of a deceased loved one appearing to a grieving person and delivering a message of consolation.

At first I thought, "What a coincidence that all these people should bring me their stories." I felt unworthy to think God might be orchestrating everything for me. It didn't occur to me that I might have a role to play in the healing of those who needed to tell their stories, and that these healing stories would help tens of thousands more who needed to hear them.

Each time someone shared their story we cried together, and each time I healed a little more as I shared the story of Jason and his messages.

It was my husband, Shawn, who first suggested I put the stories into a book that could offer people hope. Excited about the prospect, I began working on it. Then I stopped.

I was suddenly concerned about the rightness of what I was doing. Why didn't I just ask God? I think it was because I didn't have the faith that He would answer me. I put my energies back into my job as director of health, fitness and lifestyles for the local Y.M.C.A.

It was almost three years later, when I quit my job to write a children's book of rhymes, that I began to get signs to write a book of stories of heavenly intervention. One after another, eight times in all, I was shown that this was right.

Writing the book became a healing journey for me, a four year privileged task. I didn't advertise for stories, yet they came to me, by the hundreds. It was as if I was suddenly a magnet for stories about angels, and special dreams, death-bed visions and after-death communication. I was to learn things I never even imagined could be possible.

As I worked on the book, I yearned to hear my son's voice again. Five years after his death I broke down sobbing and begged God, "Please just let my son give me a hug in a dream?" That very week I had a healing dream that taught me a deep lesson. In the dream Jason was seven or eight years old, measuring only up to my chest. I was reprimanding him for something and said emphatically, "Don't do that. You could get killed!"

He looked up at me innocently and said, "But mom, death isn't forever." Jason was showing me that death is an illusion!

I finally published my book of stories called, *A Little Door, A Little Light* and was soon invited to speak at conferences and church meetings. Because of my fear of being ridiculed, I only spoke of the miraculous stories of others, and kept my story a secret. As an author I've published books on creative movement, and also some children's stories.

After one event where I'd been speaking on creative movement, people were gathered around a table where my books were displayed for sale. One lady picked up *A Little Door, A Little Light* and asked, "What's this one about?"

It was so unexpected and I was caught off guard. I swallowed, looking at the small group waiting expectantly. Apprehensively I began telling them of Jason, his death and his miraculous appearance in church. For a moment no one spoke. Then things picked up, purchases were made and people left.

I was almost packed up and ready to leave when one of the ladies reappeared, tears streaming down her face. She choked on her words, fighting for control, "I just wanted to thank you for telling your story." She told me how she'd seen her own child who'd passed away, and how her family told her never to speak of it or they'd lock her up.

Before leaving she said, "Thank you, this has been like a gift to me." I knew then why I needed to share my words and the book.

When the book, *A Little Door, A little Light*, was published, I looked back, marveling at the road I had traveled, grateful for the support of God and my husband. I thought my job was done and felt a little sad that I would no longer be collecting the beautiful stories. I was soon to learn this was not the finish.

A year after we published *A Little Door, A Little Light* a message came to me from a stranger, "You're blocking God."

"I am not," was my knee jerk reaction. Later, as I thought about the statement, I realized how true it was. I'd become preoccupied with "things of this world" and had been saying my prayers from memorization, instead of from the heart. Where before I'd been open and aware of the soft voice of God, of late I'd been simply too caught up in life to hear the soft whispers. So, it was no wonder that the next message that came from my son, did not come directly to me.

One evening, not long after the message about blocking God, a friend telephoned me. Shari has a special gift of working with energy to assist people in healing themselves. She began to speak, stuttered, started again, interrupted herself and then beat around the bush to the point of frustration. Finally she said, "You're going to find this difficult to believe, but I received five messages from Jason. He wanted me to share them with you." What made this even stranger was that Shari had never met my son. What's more, she had never had an experience of communicating with the dead, so the entire thing really shook her up.

It had been a long time since Jason had come to me, so I was awestruck by the fact he'd been trying to get through, and had resorted to contacting my friend Shari. I waited in anticipation for the words she had for me.

She told me Jason said, *"Tell my mom not to go to Calgary tomorrow."* I drew in my breath. I was planning the trip, but had not discussed it with anyone. God alone knew my plans. I stayed home.

The next message was, *"Tell my mom if she stays home she will get an important story."* I stayed and I did. I received two stories and they will be in the new book.

The third message was more personal, a puzzle that I did not understand for months. He said, *"Tell my mom to talk to my dad."* We had been divorced two years before Jason's death, and now Jason's father was living in the shadow of cancer. He needed to discuss something with me regarding our daughters and it was important that the lines of communication be opened.

The fourth message: *"Tell my mom she should write another book. It will help ease the pain for others."* It was just the right message, because I knew it was something I had wanted to do. And of course, God knew it too.

The fifth and final message was, *"Tell my mom I love her."*

I was deeply touched by the messages from Jason and knew I needed to write the follow up book to *A Little Door, A Little Light.*

It has been 16 years since Jason's death. People often write to me, especially those who've lost a child. They know I have walked the path they are just beginning. We talk. I speak to them like a big sister, and like Jason always did, I seem to find the right words to help them along a tough road. I feel privileged to have these opportunities and I am always amazed at the healing that takes place.

Isn't it all astounding?

~ *Ellie Braun-Haley*

Honoring My Dreams

If you're talented at music, that talent is of God.
If something makes your heart sing,
that's God's way of telling you it's a contribution
He wants you to make.
~ Marianne Williamson

When I looked at myself in the mirror, the image I saw was of a frazzled woman in her thirties. *I am too young to look like this*, I thought. It seemed lately that I'd been presented with one crisis after another. As a wife, with a full time job, and mother of a three-year-old daughter, life had become so busy. With taking care of others, I'd lost sight of my own dreams.

My husband, Robin, and I had been married almost eight years when we lost our second child, a boy. I'd been carrying him for almost five and a half months when the doctors discovered a serious problem. We were stunned to learn he had a heart defect, coupled with Down Syndrome. When the doctor told us his chances of survival outside the womb were impossible, we were totally devastated.

The experience of saying goodbye to a son we would never know sent our lives into a tailspin. Like most parents, we had high hopes for our new baby. Now we were being told he had to leave us. Robin and I each struggled individually to cope with the sadness. While I cried a great deal, Robin remained stoic. Thankfully, because of our ability to talk to each other about the loss of our unborn son, we managed to hold our marriage together. I loved my job; my work was fulfilling, and I felt I would manage to make it through.

Six months later, almost to the day, the company where I'd been employed for several years went through a downsizing. My position was eliminated, and I was let go. My feelings were understandably bruised. I loved the company and was a loyal employee.

I was still grieving the loss of my baby, and now had the loss of my job and the stress of unemployment to deal with. I became so drained and depressed I felt I might collapse from the mental and emotional strain.

Fortunately, I was able to find another job very quickly. However, although I was grateful for a source of steady income, the monotonous rut of going to work, preparing meals, folding laundry, and generally taking care of everyone except myself, began to slowly erode my sense of self-worth and well being.

Back when I was a teenager, I'd had aspirations of becoming a singer. I absolutely loved to sing. But, when I learned that others considered me 'good, but not good enough', I gave up on my dream. When my friends, who had enjoyed my singing, asked me to perform at parties, I started mumbling lame excuses. 'What was the point?' I reasoned silently. 'It's not going to get me anywhere'. For some reason, I no longer felt I had the *right* to sing, and stopped altogether.

A few years later, as I entered adulthood, I set my sights on a lucrative future in writing. I loved it, and knew I had a knack for it, so I set about attaining a degree. However, after a two-year college diploma in writing failed to produce a job in that field, I gave up on that dream as well. Needing to earn a living, I turned to the more attainable goal of becoming a secretary.

The lifestyle I had been living had drained my life force, and I felt a strong inner urge to make some changes. I've always known that dreams can reveal things about our deepest wishes. I began to have dreams where I was at a microphone belting out songs, but in each dream there was a technical glitch. The power would short out, leaving me silent, and voiceless.

I realized my dream was telling me that my own power had been cut short. The way to gain it back would be to find an outlet for my voice – it was time to start singing again. I became determined to prove to myself that *I could be heard*. I knew in my heart this was the missing piece, or *glitch* in my dream, that once repaired, would bring joy and energy back into my life. I began to get excited!

I shared my dream with Robin, and as always he was very supportive. He understood and respected my creative leanings, and urged me to go for it. To start the ball rolling, I went to a local music shop and put up an ad that said, "Singer Available." Then, went home, and held my breath.

Within the first week, I began to get responses. The second call I got was from an established country rock band looking for a singer to reignite their sound. I was excited when they discovered I was just what they'd been looking for. After only one session singing with the band, I began to feel my enthusiasm for life returning.

Every Friday night I was at practice without fail. I found that the more I sang, the more my wounded self-esteem began to heal. I loved it so much, and found myself moving, thinking, and *feeling* with a renewed sense of self.

I sang with the band for two wonderful years. Then, when my second daughter was born, the demands on my time made it impossible to sustain. Before long, I once again found the same feelings of spiritual lethargy creeping back in. Robin was working shift work, and arranging an evening out was difficult. I felt guilty for wanting time away from the children, and so once again, I put my needs on hold.

Pretty soon, just like before, my dreams began to communicate a need for a creative outlet. This time it was writing. My dreams were forcing me to realize, that no matter what my personal obligations might be, my need for creative personal expression had to be honored.

When I found an online community magazine that was looking for articles, I found an outlet for my creative urges. I was given my own column, and the thrill of seeing my articles published each week was wonderful.

These days, I fill the time on my commute to and from work with loud, joyous singing. My husband jokingly threatens to have the windows of our car tinted so other drivers don't think me wild. I now sing with a band again, and my dreams show me that I'm right on track creatively.

I've heard many women my age lament about how, with family demands, their creative aspirations seem to have slipped away. They wonder out loud what they might have become if they had chosen another path.

As it happens, I am not one of those women. I have learned that I don't have to put my dreams on the back burner, while my children grow up; in fact, it works better for everyone if I don't. Instead, the energy I derive from self-fulfillment, allows me to give back to my children, two-fold. I manage my treasured moments here and there to write my thoughts, and keep alive my creative spirit.

My dreams are what keep that sacred part of me alive. I never realized until recently, how through living and fulfilling my own creative aspirations, I am able to give my children the best I have to offer. And by showing them how to live their dreams and care for themselves emotionally and spiritually, they will benefit for the rest of their lives.

~ *Brenda Chisholm*

From Spark to Flame

*If you want your life to be more rewarding,
you have to change the way you think.*
~ Oprah Winfrey

When my 19 year old daughter was back in Grade 3, she and her classmates were given a small pot with a bean seed to plant. Green string beans, it seems, are pretty hardy and the perfect seed to use when encouraging green thumbs in young children.

That same plant was also a most unexpected source of understanding and insight for me.

Once the bean plants had sprouted and flowered on the classroom window sills, their teacher allowed the kids to carefully transfer the precious cargo from school to home. Once home, Shanna scouted around for the perfect location and settled on a sunny south sill. Then she proudly declared, "Soon I can feed the whole family!"

Shanna's sisters were envious and even our cat looked intrigued, which should have been a warning to me, because when I woke up the next morning I saw that the bean plant had been maliciously knocked off the window sill and ripped from it's pot. Its leaves were frayed and, except for a limp thread of stem that still connected the roots to the flowering top, it was quite unrecognizable from the day before.

The plant, it seemed, was a goner.

I dreaded telling Shanna, but as I gently began to explain that the bean plant had to be put in the compost, her reaction was not what I expected. She said, "Everything will be okay Mom, the plant will get better."

Without giving it a second thought, she ran for the first aid kit from the bathroom. She returned with gauze, a tongue depressor, bandages and a deep belief that her pathetic looking, near-dead bean plant would live, thrive and even produce food! I had mixed emotions, knowing that she was postponing the plant's inevitable trip to our compost bin, but I went along with it and helped her with her first aid.

Days later, to my absolute surprise, the bean plant was standing tall and looking perky. We removed the bandages and discovered a protruding hump in the stem where the near-fatal break had been. We were also amazed to see that the one and only bean had become plump, and the claw marks that had scarred it were barely visible.

I don't know why I didn't think the cat might go for a second round, because it surely did, and this time I was the one who ran for the first aid kit! I carefully applied a cast made of everything from cotton and gauze to colored band aids with "ouch" written on them. When my medical work was done, I whispered a little something to the heavens.

Just one week later we removed the bandages, and again we barely found evidence of the attack. There was even a new sliver of green where a second bean was sprouting. I was astounded. Shanna was not. She expected nothing less.

Back to its window sill the war torn little plant went. This time we built a fortress of heavy books around it to keep it safe.

That Thanksgiving I set the table with more fanfare than usual.

It looked beautiful. The beans were carefully divided by 5, which meant we each got two, claw marks and all. We agreed they were the best green beans we had ever eaten!

My daughter didn't really understand my exuberance over what happened with the bean plant.

In my work as a youth motivator, I interact with kids and teens who all desperately need people to believe in them. Now, no matter what I have been told about children and their behavior, I make the effort to see each one, *no exceptions*, with the eyes and heart of my daughter. I want to live the example she set with her strong belief in the recovery of her poor broken, beaten up bean plant.

I wonder if it's a coincidence that later that same week, I stumbled upon a most appropriate quote by the Italian poet, Dante (1265-1351): "From a little spark, may burst a mighty flame."

Especially if you believe...!

~ *Monique Howat*

5

The Miracle of Birth

"Bringing a child into the world
is the greatest act of hope there is."

— Louise Hart

Building the Safe Bridge

Yet again, my husband and I were consulting with fertility specialists to try to solve the question of why I couldn't stay pregnant.

By now I had conceived and lost five times. I had also conceived and carried my son, who blessedly had just turned three. I knew how it felt to conceive, to feel the subtle electric shift in my belly. In many ways, my conceptions seemed similar to descriptions I'd read of near-death experiences. I could feel the whisper of the veil between worlds gently draw back to allow a little soul to circle me and make contact. The movement was so slight that it was initially easy to miss, but over time and with so many conceptions I finally learned to recognize it.

One moonlit night, I felt a gentle tap at my womb's door and I became pregnant again. Pregnancy was a punishing, grueling marathon for me; pregnancy with my son had been life-threatening, his birth an agonizing and dramatic forty-two hours.

I had held off interventions for longer than anyone had thought possible, but in the end my body gave out and they pulled him out of me. It took three years for me to fully regain my footing. I was viscerally aware of the thin, dangerous line I walked in order to accompany my next child into the world. But I had no choice; my little one was sitting patiently on the other side, invisible but palpable in my quiet moments.

After surviving a harrowing first trimester filled with hazy, frightening days, I knew I needed to take a different strategy this time. I had had enough of living in constant fear. I wanted to spend more time building intentional connections with the baby. This took enormous courage. Because I had lost so often before, it was very difficult to open myself up to my baby and to stay that way. I hoped, though, that this would be how I could see my way through to the other side of a pregnancy and a safe birth.

I contacted a local wellness clinic and signed up for a course on hypnosis for childbirth. Each session involved going into a deep state of relaxed awareness, and then into a self-hypnotized state. While in this state we practiced connecting with the baby, signaling what we needed from our partners and turning sensation on and off to different parts of our bodies. There were many documented benefits to using hypnosis for childbirth – pain reduction, decreasing the length of labor, promoting a relaxed and confident birth.

I practiced every night before bed, working to keep my anxiety at bay, and learned to move into self-hypnosis. I visualized myself as a vibrant, white lotus cradling a strong and healthy baby. I slid my consciousness down my throat into my belly to curl around my baby; similar to the way she had curled into my belly and settled there when she first arrived so many months ago. It felt like I was resting next to her, ever so gently. I wove a light pink membrane of safety and love around her. I had always known, instinctively, that she was a girl, but it was still nice to feel that confirmation of her feminine energy.

As the weeks passed and the baby grew inside me, she remained healthy but, as had happened with my first pregnancy, I developed life-threatening complications. Physically I became severely limited in what I could do, and my terror grew. Now, more than ever, I needed the extra strength I had learned to access through hypnosis. I tapped into my reserves and I made full use of the quiet power there.

Several times a day I practiced hypnotizing myself, and I worked on sending encouraging messages deep into my core.

When the midwife found that the baby was breech at 34 weeks, I connected with the baby and encouraged her to turn. Within three days, she shifted to a head-down position. Shortly before the birth, she ended up in a posterior position, facing up instead of towards my spine. I was told it could result in a much more difficult and painful birth. Once again I reached inside and asked her to shift. Again, she quietly moved around to the optimal birthing position. I refused to allow myself any more heady doubt or breathy fear – when I settled inwards, I was calm. So was the baby.

Her eventual emergency induction at birth was intense, but had a flow and primitive grace to it as well. I insisted that there be no distracting conversations, music, or instructions. I melted into my body to such a strong degree that in some ways I felt like my essence helped ease her through my birth canal, guiding her in her molding movements.

I sat on a birthing ball for the first part of the birth, my head in my husband's lap, listening to my hypnosis guidance compact disc on a continuous loop. As I progressed and my contractions became increasingly fierce, I felt like I might split apart and memories of my son's traumatic birth came flooding back. I shook uncontrollably, drenched in sweat, and focused all of my energy on staying in my body, in a most primal way.

In the end, this birth experience was very different from my first – just as painful, but much shorter and so much more my own. Though there was a strong chance of complications and even of death, I didn't die, and neither did my baby. She came out of me quickly and didn't cry as she was toweled off and placed on my belly. I murmured, "Hi sweetie, welcome to the world!" leaned back on the pillow and burst into tears. We had both held on so hard and for so long – the release I felt through my deep sobs was overwhelmingly intense.

She blinked and mewed softly as I nuzzled into this sweet soul. This sticky, delicate, familiar creature, my daughter, was finally here. We called her Shanna Faith: Shanna, a Celtic name meaning wisdom, and Faith, symbolizing the fierce belief it took to bring her safely over the threshold into this world. Welcome to the world Shanna!

~ *Catherine Stafford*

Before You

For Melanie

Before you
There was Washington, D.C.:
The crisp click of high-heeled shoes
In gleaming subway stations,
A window office overlooking the Potomac.
Next to you, empty
As a cellophane box.

Before you
There were stylish business suits
And cocktail parties,
Committee meetings, and bound reports.
One giggle from you
Makes them all laughable.

Before you
There were reams of academic research,
Published papers, and names on programs.
One dimpled grin
Turns them all to dust.

Before you,
Everything mattered so much,
And came to so little.
Now nothing matters much at all anymore
Compared to you.

~ Laura Reave

If He Were a She

Your children are not your children.
They are the sons and daughters
of Life's longing for itself.
~ Kahlil Gibran

When I was pregnant with my second child, it was no secret that I hoped for a girl. I already had one beautiful son, Nathaniel, and I believed that a daughter would complete my family perfectly.

When, baby boy, Lee, was born, I found I loved him just as much as my first born. Even so, at times, I would dream of how my life would be different if he were a she, and then I'd feel a little ashamed. I should be satisfied with a healthy child of either gender.

Soon after Lee was born, a good male friend, who knew of my hopes of having a girl, said to me: "There aren't enough sensitive men in the world; that's why you were meant to have boys." This helped me rise above my longing for a baby girl. I thanked him for that beautiful sentiment and accepted his message as truth. I even repeated that line in my head many times over those first few years of motherhood: a small part of me still didn't accept it.

As a kid, I was a typical girl who took ballet, *aspired to be a dancer,* loved to color and play with dolls. It seems comical now that my cousin, Rona and I would spend many weekends playing with our dolls, my Ken and her Alan. We didn't have a Barbie between us, but somehow that didn't seem to cramp our creative play. We would still dress them up in their outfits and make up stories about their dates. Strange that, as we played, I always imagined growing up to be the mom of a little girl.

Naturally, my sons grew into typical, physically active boys. I would play with them as best I could, getting down on all fours and doing whatever boys do. I was amazed how boys instinctively make car and truck sounds. Girls aren't equipped with that sort of programming. How did these noises come out of little boys before they even knew what it was they were copying?

By the time the boys were six and three, my husband and I separated. Eventually a special man entered my life. Dave had two daughters from his previous marriage: Cheryl, six like my Nathaniel, and Jana, nine. The four kids became friends as the new family bonded. The girls loved to treat Lee like their personal doll, always dressing him up in crazy outfits.

When the girls came to visit every other weekend and at holiday time, I tried to soak up all the girl energy I could. I braided their hair: they braided Nathaniel's. They made up his face and donned him in girl clothes, complete with padded bra. Was this the daughter I was missing, I laughed to myself? I took photos and thought about the fun of showing them to his future girlfriend or bride. *Then, sadly, the girls would return home.*

Thank goodness, the boys didn't show any interest in playing hockey, because I definitely would have been at a loss. Instead, gymnastics, trampoline and music were their extra curricular activities of choice. All of these were right up my alley because I inhabited a world of performing arts. In my work for over twenty years I had been doing children's mime, clown and mask shows all over the province of Ontario.

When Nathaniel was eight years old, after he showed some interest in being part of my show, I choreographed a mask piece for the two of us to perform together. This gave us a new way to connect that summer and we had fun with the crowds at Kingston's annual *Buskers' Rendezvous*. We didn't make a lot of money, but he just loved performing. I realized then performing was in his genes.

One day, when Lee was eight years old, he asked about taking ballet. I'm still not sure where his idea originated, but ironically, the movie, 'Billy Elliot', came out just months later. I had been a dance major in University, until I decided to veer towards theatre. When I studied mime, I knew I'd found my niche: the perfect balance of dance and theatre. I agreed to take Lee to a trial dance class to see if his interest was real. His love of ballet grew and before long he added jazz dance to his repertoire. Soon it dawned on me that my connection to my sons was deepening. We were bonding through the arts, through wonderful, creative and spiritual art forms. That "girl void" I'd been feeling was practically gone. As for Lee, his confidence was growing and after two years of classes, he was accepted to the Quinte professional ballet school. He attended for the next six months and then decided to return home because he missed us so much.

Now Nathaniel is a professional magician and juggler and has created his own original shows. He performs at a variety of venues, has won international awards for his magic, and aspires to tour and perform internationally.

More recently, I have given up performing professionally due to my health and I think about our journey. I'll always be very proud of all my children, and after years of being a mom, I know in my heart that gender is completely irrelevant. It's finding a way to connect with your children that matters. It seems silly that it took me so long to accept my destiny to be surrounded by males. Many times I have told people, with a chuckle, that this is my fate – even our pets are male. It's been my special honor to bring these caring, giving, sensitive beings to our world.

~ *Dalia Gesser*

Love Has No Boundaries

The dream came again. There was the same little four-year-old boy, and the same little two-year-old girl. When I awoke, it was with the familiar feeling of love and wonder that always followed. The dream was part of a series of dreams that began when I was 25 years old, and living for a brief period at home with my parents in Paisley Scotland. From the dreams, I knew these children were living in Canada. I began to feel that I should go there, but then I'd think, "I have no money. It's just not possible!" I received some inner nudges that told me to live as if I were actually in Canada. Each day as I walked to work, I'd pretend that I was breathing Canadian air and that I was looking at Canadian countryside, until I began to believe that I was walking on Canadian soil.

One day, out of the blue, I received an important letter from an uncle in Switzerland. In it he said: "I've decided you should go to Canada, because I think it's important for your education. I'm going to start sending you magazines about Canada, and I'm buying you a round-trip ticket. That way if you get there and you find you don't like it, you can return home anytime within one year."

This was like a miracle! It seemed the visualizing was working and meanwhile I continued to have these very strong dreams about the two children. The feeling that I was linked to them was getting stronger and stronger.

My first instinct was to go to Vancouver in western Canada, but some family friends were living in Ottawa, in the province of Ontario, and they offered me a place to stay. Then I realized that in the dreams, it felt like these children were in the eastern part of Canada, not the west. I decided to live in Ottawa for a year and then decide about heading west. I arrived in Ottawa in August 1967. It was Canada's centennial year!

I stayed with the Ottawa family, found a nursing job at the Civic Hospital, and worked there for the year I'd planned. I had a boyfriend for a while, and when we broke up, it seemed the obvious time to go on with my plan. Just when I'd made up my mind, an old friend, a nurse from Scotland, contacted me and came to Ottawa for a visit. She was renting a house in Hamilton, Ontario and was looking for a roommate. She encouraged me to come for a short visit.

When my bus arrived in Hamilton I was still feeling a bit sad about the boyfriend. She said, "We need to go out and have a good time."

We got ourselves all dressed up, and although we had no idea where we were going, I kept telling her, "Don't worry; I'll know it when we get there." We caught a cab downtown. As we drove along, I heard some Jazz music coming from a hotel through the open window of the cab, so I said to her, "This is it; this is where we get out!"

No wonder I was attracted to the music! A band from Scotland, *The Metro Stompers*, was playing. There was no doubt we were meant to be there.

We barely got seated when I felt an invisible hand grab me by the scruff of the neck and turn my head around. A voice within me said, "Look, there is the man you are going to marry." I saw a good-looking guy at a table across the room from me, and it was almost like I wasn't allowed to take my eyes away from him. I immediately believed the voice I'd heard. I absolutely knew that this man I hadn't even spoken to yet, was going to be my husband.

Within a few seconds his eyes turned towards me. He came over to our table, introduced himself as Bob, and started to chat. We ended up spending the entire evening with him, and when it was time to call it a night, he drove the two of us home.

When we began dating, he told me that before he had even introduced himself, he knew I was the girl he was going to marry.

My return ticket to Scotland expired by October, so I decided to go home for a visit. Bob was anxious to meet my family and joined me on the trip. During the flight, he said, "I have something to tell you. I was married before, and I have two children."

He expected a surprised reaction, but instead I turned to him and said, "I know, a little boy and a little girl!" Then I told him about the dreams, and how I'd been waiting to solve the mystery of these dream-children.

"Are they real? Who are they and where do they live?" I asked. It seemed I had been traveling toward Bob and his children all my life.

While we were visiting with my parents, he asked me to marry him, and of course I said yes! We became engaged, thinking we would get married in a year. Then my parents suggested, "Why go back and wait a year to get married? Why don't you get married here in Scotland?" I'd only known Bob for six weeks, but he was all for it, so I agreed too. A few days later, with my dad performing the ceremony, we were married.

After a honeymoon in Ireland, we returned home to Canada. First, I met his parents. As soon as I saw his father, I began to cry, because I recognized him as someone I would love very much. I just hugged him and hugged him. Shortly after that, I met my two stepchildren. By this time, the little boy was almost six, and the little girl had just turned four. When Bob brought them through the door, I recognized them instantly as the children from my dreams. The strong bond of affection was already there. They were so happy to see me, and we hugged, not as strangers, but as if reunited. We shared such a strong connection from the heart, and so much love.

For several years we looked forward to spending every second weekend and some holidays with the children. When their step-sister and step-brother were born we all became one big happy family.

Eventually their mother remarried and life changed dramatically for us all. We were no longer allowed to see the children, talk to them, or have any contact with them, whatsoever. They moved away and we felt the agony of not even knowing where in the world they were.

My husband became severely depressed, was unable to work and had to be hospitalized for a while. He despaired of ever seeing his children again. Then my dream of the children returned. The doorbell would ring, my husband would open the door and there standing before us were the children, now adults, with big smiles on their faces. When I would tell Bob about the dream, his spirits would pick up for a short time, then the depression would hit once again. I had this recurring dream many times during the next 22 years. It always came when Bob was feeling the lowest, and because of the wonderful outcome of my first dreams of the children, it would always encourage and uplift us both.

One memorable day the telephone rang and it was my step-daughter on the other end of the line. As she talked, I had a hard time choking back the tears. I told her about the dream and how I had never doubted for one second that I would see her again.

When Bob talked to his daughter for the first time in 22 years, there was a lump in his throat, and tears of joy streaming down his face. Several days later, we experienced the dream come true. The doorbell rang and two familiar smiling faces stood before us.

What a reunion that was!

We learned that life had not been easy for the children, but the memory of the love we gave them in childhood had helped to give them courage during some difficult times. They were both married with young children of their own and were now free to make their own decisions.

We feel so blessed each time the children and grandchildren come for a visit. I realize that part of my role as step-mother is to teach them all I know about forgiveness, that time can heal the deepest wounds and best of all, love has no boundaries.

~ *Sybil Barbour*

I Will always Hear Georgie

In my heart I will always hear Georgie
Although I do not know
Of the boys she's kissed
The songs she's sung
The color of her dress on prom night
The days when she laughed.. and laughed.. and laughed
Years pass
Oh … how many memories I've missed?

Although
I cannot hear
Georgie crying
I cannot hear
The silence of the past
I cannot hear
Georgie crying
My love will always last

In my heart I will always hear Georgie
Although I cannot say
Where she is now
That her favorite color is lapis blue
That she drinks wine from a silver goblet or a plastic mug

That she always carries an umbrella
Minutes are days and suddenly
My eyes open ... wet

In my heart I will always hear Georgie
Although the memories appear like old reels of film
Sunny days
Blankets, beach hats, orange flowered bikinis
Ah .. I can feel the water on my toes and she smiles at me
Belly button giggles with purple popsicle stains
from ear to ear
The sand bakes us gently
Shovels, pails, castles
Castles to hide in

Although I cannot hear Georgie crying

I know
Bruises, bumps, sprained ankles
Payton house sunburns
Cub cars whizzzzzzzzzzzzzing along
Bees in Victoria Park
Boiled eggs, Chicken noodle soup, Dimpflmeier
bread and butter
Camp Ki-Wi-Y phone calls, home-made packages
Random Harvest, Elwy Yost, The Sound of Music
Early ... brrrrrrrrrr ... morning hockey practices

I can say
I was there
To listen
To know
To say
To feel
To breathe

And I can hear Georgie

~ *Sheila Good*

Note to a Birth Mother

You gave birth to him. I got to be his mother.

Because of a selfless choice you made, I got to experience the wonders no mother should ever take for granted … rocking chair lullabies, wiping sad tears, sharing giggles, hugs and kisses. Exchanging words of love. The excitement of seeing him learn new things.

Because of a selfless choice you made, he had the opportunity to become a first-class athlete. He's bi-lingual. He attended university. He studied for a creative career. He traveled extensively.

Today he is a very successful businessman. He has lots of friends and a lovely partner.

You gave him life. You gave him the chance to reach for the stars – and he did. Thank you.

~ *Bonita O'Neill*

The True Nature of Love

I guess I always knew that expectant Moms worry. They worry about the condition of the baby they long to see, but can only feel, moving and growing deep inside them. They quit smoking, they refuse even a sip of wine, and only the healthiest food is good enough to send in to nourish that little person.

What surprised me was quite a different worry that landed early in my second pregnancy.

Kristin was three: first daughter, first grand-daughter. Blonde and beautiful, chubby and smart. She talked early and when she laughed it came from a place deep in her belly. Hearing it made everyone around her laugh too. My husband, Cal, and I loved her so much we thought we would burst.

So what could I possibly worry about? Why would I think a second pregnancy would not present us with another special gift?

It was a question that repeated itself in my head – one I was ashamed to articulate. "How could we possibly love our second child as much as we loved Kristin?"

It niggled at the edge of my consciousness and even dawned on me again as I breathed through my pain on the drive to the hospital.

This labor was much longer than my first. When our new daughter arrived, I was just glad to have her out of me. They whisked her away quickly; we barely had a chance to look at her and then they moved me to recovery.

A few hours later, a nurse wheeled my bed along a corridor toward the semi-private room that would be ours for the next couple of days. I was getting really anxious to see our baby.

I raised my head instinctively and saw a man holding a bundle in a yellow blanket. It was Cal. He had the biggest, silliest grin on his face, and he was walking toward me. As he arrived, the nurse kindly stopped my rolling bed and Cal bent over. He pulled back the yellow blanket and showed me his prize.

When her quizzical eyes met mine I felt an immediate physical reaction. I'm not talking a little sensation here. What I mean is … I felt a huge quake of thunder roll through me. It actually knocked me back. I know now that what I felt was the surprise of recognition. The wave that passed through me was the reclaiming of the infinite love I already had for this soul I've always known.

Colleen had arrived; her name was chosen by her older sister. Both girls are beautiful, and as different as night and day, even though they share the same warped sense of humour.

When I'm around expectant Moms, I'll often ask them about their worries. Sometimes I share this story, sometimes I don't. I wouldn't want to spoil, for them, what Colleen taught me about the true nature of love that day of her birth, when we were reunited.

There is enough love to go around. The well of love is bottomless, and best of all, love is eternal!

~ Judy Prang

Life's Miracles

On May 14, 2005, I was walking around Wal-Mart, preparing for my little one's arrival. I stopped occasionally in the aisles, feeling slight cramps. It dawned on me, while I was deciding which diaper cream would be best, that I might be in the first stage of labor.

At 37 weeks I stood there not knowing that the umbilical cord had wrapped around my baby's neck, and that he was in deep distress.

I arrived home, where I packed a bag for my stay in the hospital, thinking that in a few short hours I would be holding my child, just as I had my firstborn. My daughter, Zaahira had been three weeks early too, and thank God there had been no complications.

Minutes later, in the washroom, I felt a snap inside of me. It was then I knew something was seriously wrong. I got myself to the door and called out to my husband. We headed for the car and immediately sped to the hospital.

In the emergency room, the pain was unbearable. All I could say, over and over, was, "Someone please help me!" My husband stood at my side, helpless to do anything – except panic. It felt like days to me, but within an hour, they delivered my baby, by Caesarean Section.

I awoke to learn my baby was fine. An incredible feeling of relief and joy swept through me, but unfortunately this was short lived. A few hours later, I was told that little Zaahid's breathing stopped every time he fell asleep. And to further complicate things, one of the nurses noticed some signs of seizure activity. Because we live in the small town of Welland, Ontario in Canada, the pediatrician on call decided it would be best for Zaahid to be transferred to a hospital with better neonatal care facilities. I was to remain behind at Welland General until I was rested enough for the trip.

All of the hospitals were fully occupied, except for the Children's Hospital of Western Ontario, in London. They brought my little boy, weighing just under 5 pounds, to me in a bed especially designed for the 4 hour ambulance ride. I kissed him and they assured me that things were fine. Despite all the medication I was on, I did not sleep that night until I was sure my son had reached London safely. I was certain that everything would be alright once he got there and that my tiny, beautiful boy would be home in no time.

I received another shock when shortly after he was admitted, the pediatrician called to notify me of a mass in my baby's heart. They needed permission to give Zaahid a blood transfusion, because his red blood cell count was dangerously low, and to perform tests to investigate the mass.

I sat there in my hospital bed, in disbelief, trying to piece this puzzling situation together. My husband had already left for home to help my mother-in-law with my daughter. My heart was breaking, because I had never spent a single night away from her since her birth, two years and three months earlier.

Next I learned that, along with the unexplained mass in Zaahid's heart, he had two heart murmurs and extremely low red blood cells. An MRI showed damage to the brain, due to lack of oxygen during labor. All of this was being explained to me while Zaahid was halfway across the province. Although I had just had major surgery, there was nothing that could stop me from going to be with him.

The next day I was released, then traveled the four hours by car to reach Zaahid, shivering from exhaustion on the hot summer day. I remember hoping the Tylenol would keep me intact until I could reach the Pediatric Critical Care Unit. Once there, I took a hotel room as my base.

Zaahid was in the PCCU for one week. While there, we met the cardiologist, neurologist, hematologist and the rest of the team that was working with my son. It was overwhelming, but very reassuring to see how well cared for he was.

I was on an emotional roller coaster, one moment fine and confident, the next an emotional wreck. All the while, I felt the strength and endurance God placed within me, along with my family's optimism and genuine support.

In the PCCU, Zaahid had the doctors mind-boggled. The second cardio-echo showed the mass in his heart had disappeared; they thought it went up to his brain, but that wasn't the case. The second MRI showed less brain damage than the first, but his red blood cell count had steadily decreased. He needed another transfusion.

My trust in God strengthened. Within a few short days Zaahid went from needing constant watch, to such an improved state, that it amazed the doctors. We were moved up to the seventh floor, where children under the age of one are cared for. Zaahid still needed oxygen and a feeding tube, because he wasn't taking to the bottle. I held on to the hope of nursing him as soon as he could be weaned from the oxygen tube.

I was in for another disappointment. The team monitoring him was afraid that Zaahid would not be able to swallow, because they knew my first born had had 'tracheomalasia', a higher then usual cleft palate. Until he could be monitored by the feeding and swallowing team, they would not allow me to breastfeed.

This was heartbreaking for me. I remembered the bond that nursing brought with my first child. He was already on blood thinning medication because of the clot, iron supplement because of anemia, and Phenobarbital seizure medication. I didn't want him to have formula too. I felt that if I could just breastfeed him, we could overcome anything.

A few days later, the occupational therapist confirmed my fear. She said that Zaahid would not be able to breastfeed because he was unable to co-ordinate latching on and suckling. It was three weeks since his birth, and I just wanted to go home, where I could care for him myself. To get home, we needed him off the feeding tube, so I told them to start giving him bottles. Meanwhile I would continue to try nursing him.

At the same time, there were many other parents with sick babies who were struggling along and trying to stay positive. Their courage helped me to stay strong. The constant prayers and support that surrounded me drowned out any hopelessness that came up. Within a day or two, Zaahid did start breastfeeding, astonishing everyone. By the end of the week, he was off the blood thinners and was fully breastfeeding. When we learned they were sending us home, I was overjoyed!

At three months, we were able to wean him off the Phenobarbital and by six months we were shaking our heads wondering how our healthy and beautiful looking boy could ever have been ill.

Today, I can look back at this experience and see how it has strengthened me as a mother and a woman. What started out as a nightmare, became a series of amazing miracles. I now have a deep appreciation for the healing ability of our bodies. When I think of the mass in Zaahid's heart that disappeared, the brain damage that corrected itself, and how he learned to breastfeed three weeks after birth, I now believe that with an optimistic view, anything is possible!

~ Sabrina Mohamedali

6

Life's Most Interesting Moments

Shanna's Gift

Like most children, my eight year old daughter, Shanna, asked for things every single time she saw something cute at a friend's house, on TV, or in stores. We were young parents struggling to make our mortgage payments, so each time she asked, "Can you buy me that mommy ... please?" my standard answer was always, "I'm sorry, Shanna, we simply can't afford it."

Finally she stopped asking.

One day I heard my 10 year old daughter shouting for me to come quickly. I was sure I heard her say that Shanna was stealing money from my purse! I raced to the kitchen where I found my purse on the floor with Shanna's hand still in it ... frozen in a moment of pure dread.

I was utterly shocked and horribly disappointed. I wondered where she had learned to steal. Did she really think she could get away with it?

By now Shanna was crying hard and looking as traumatized as me. I managed to remain calm while I gently, but firmly, asked her, "How could you take something that isn't yours?"

Through her sobs she managed to say, "I didn't ... honest, Mommy. I'm not taking anything."

"Well then," I asked accusingly, "what are you doing?"

I was stunned as she explained while still sobbing, "You always say you can't buy stuff 'cuz you're broke. I was *putting* $5.00 in your purse, so you'd have some money."

That remarkably sweet gesture became even more heartfelt when she confessed she had been making a monthly deposit of $5.00 into my purse for over a year. She then asked, "Has it been helping, Mommy? Does it make you smile?"

I dropped to the floor with her and I squeezed my eyes shut because I was crying so hard. I held and rocked my adorable, thoughtful daughter, hoping I could freeze the moment and make it last. Shanna stayed cuddled in my arms for as long as she could, before announcing she needed to go because she had "things to do".

Over the next decade or so, Shanna carried out more covert missions. She continually inspires me as a mom and in my work as a self-esteem youth motivator.

Am I smiling? Absolutely beaming!

~ *Monique Howat*

A Hairdresser in Training

"Mother of God, what have you done?"

My grandmother stood in the doorway of my parent's bedroom. Her scream startled me; I dropped the scissors I had been using.

"Grammy", I asked. "What's the matter?" "Why are you upset? I was only playing hairdresser. See, I cut Omer's hair and my own, just like I watched Aunt Elissa do, when she cut Kathy's hair."

My four-year old mind could not understand her reaction over what I had done. I was so pleased with the results. I had been planning this for some time. I knew where my mom kept the scissors, in her suitcase under her bed. I knew I would have time to do the job if I skipped my nap, because my grandmother would be watching TV. I was so excited. I would be a real hairdresser. I had watched my aunt cut my sister's hair at least a million times!

Grammy ignored my questions and instead stood in shock and disbelief, as she noticed the deep cuts on my brother's head, as well as the blood on the blanket in his crib. I only saw the outcome of my hard work. I could not grasp why she was not proud of me.

I was proud of me. My brother had remained quiet and still as I trimmed his hair. I think he found it a bit entertaining. I know he liked the attention. Usually, I was dragging him around the apartment, taking his toys, feeding him leftovers. He was like one of my baby dolls. I had cut their hair and no one seemed to care. After all, I needed to practice first.

I heard another loud scream. My Mom had come into the room. Her scream frightened my brother. He started to cry and then everything got louder and louder. All of the commotion scared me and I started to cry too. I am not sure if it was because I was frightened or because of the unknown; perhaps a punishment for my actions was on its way.

A horrified expression came over my Mother's face as she saw my beautiful blonde curls lying in a pile at my feet and my little head, almost bald, with one little curl hanging in the back.

She bent down, scooped me up in her arms, and reassured me. Or was she reassuring herself that she could fix the problem? All it would take to rectify the situation was a call to my aunt, a car ride to Massachusetts, a new hairstyle … and everything would be fine.

More than thirty-two years later, I faced my own past folly, when my four-year old daughter, Tiffany, decided to play hairdresser, herself. Just like me, she practiced on her dolls by trimming their hair. Once she mastered the concept, she experimented on herself, cutting her bangs until they nearly disappeared into the top of her head. As she twirled around the room, showing off her new hairstyle, I had all I could do to maintain my composure. Vacillating between laughter and tears, I scooped my little sweetie up into my arms, knowing I could fix it. Tiffany's Godmother was a hairdresser with plenty of experience in the hair repair department. We would soon be zooming to her hair salon, where Tiffany would get a new hairstyle, a hug from me and everything would be fine.

I learned a long time ago that given enough time, hair does indeed, grow back.

~ *Karen Marie Arel*

About the Author

Darlene Montgomery is a writer, editor and respected authority on dreams who speaks to groups and organizations on uplifting subjects. Her first book published in November 1999, *Dream Yourself Awake,* chronicles the journey she took to discover her own divine mission using dreams, waking dreams and intuition.

As a consultant she helped compile two of the famous Chicken Soup books. Her stories have appeared in *Chicken Soup for the Parent's Soul* and *Chicken Soup for the Canadian Soul,* The WTN website, *Vitality Magazine* and *Synchronicity Magazine.* Darlene's recent book media campaign took her across Canada and the U.S. where she appeared on national television and radio shows, including Michael Coren Live, Rogers Daytime, CH TV, Breakfast Television, The Patty Purcell Show, The Life Station and more. As well, Darlene operates her own public relations firm, helping to promote authors and experts.

For more on Darlene and her work visit: www.lifedreams.org.

Other Books by *Darlene Montgomery*

Dream Yourself Awake

This autobiography reads like a spiritual mystery. A question asked of the author by a mysterious guide sets her on a journey to uncover the source of her deep spiritual illness and leads her to discover the one deep truth that needs to be understood in order to be healed. Throughout the story, hundreds of personal dreams act as clues to solve the mystery, leading to the personal revelation of the author.

Dreams are a natural homing device residing in the heart of soul. Many of us are aware of a yearning or sense of destiny, purpose or mission we must find before our life is complete. In *Dream Yourself Awake*, Darlene Montgomery tells the story behind the search for her own mission in a series of dreams, waking dreams and inner experiences. As we share her journey, we will discover how to use these same tools to see beyond the illusions of the mind, and travel straight to the heart of our divine purpose.

First in the Series,

Conscious Women— Conscious Lives

Powerful & Transformational Stories of Healing Body Mind & Soul

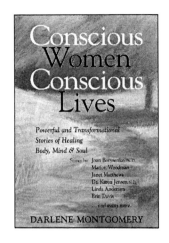

In this extraordinary collection of personal revelation, women share their deepest and heart-felt experiences of healing from loss, illness, and accident. These stories show how the journey of facing some of life's greatest obstacles can be followed by a joyous emergence from the darkness of despair, and a return to the light of life, love and new wisdom.

These true stories, written by women, for women, help open the heart, heal the spirit, and bring peace of mind during some of life's most challenging times. As each author brings a treasure from her own rich experience, she contributes to the pool of wisdom we share on this planet of how each of us can meet our greatest fears to rise again with wisdom, grace and courage. Whatever challenges you presently face, these stories offer hope, reassurance, comfort and proud examples of the resilient nature and courage of women.

Compiled by Darlene Montgomery, author of *Dream Yourself Awake* and associate editor and publicist of *Chicken Soup for the Parent's Soul* and the best-selling, *Chicken Soup for the Canadian Soul* every story is original and every one true. Many have been written explicitly for this unique collection and are from all across North America.

It is a book filled with messages of hope that only women can provide to other women.

Second in the Series,

Conscious Women— Conscious Lives

Women Share More Life-Transforming Stories of Healing, Triumphing Over Death and Scaling the Heights to Achieve Their Greatest Dreams

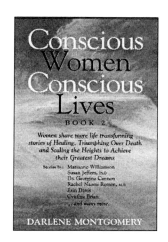

The second in the series, *Conscious Women-Conscious Lives: Book Two*, offers more extraordinary stories of healing and transformation by some of North America's leading women authorities on healing, spirituality and body mind wisdom. Each story is true and each brings healing and comfort. These stories show how the journey of facing some of life's greatest obstacles can be followed by a joyous emergence from the darkness of despair, and a return to the light of life, love and new wisdom.

Each story shows the resilient spirit of women, and that in our greatest trials are our greatest opportunities. Erin Davis shares a heart warming tale of how an inspirational poem sparked the awareness of her greater purpose in life as a renowned radio host. Marianne Williamson, shares a humorous tale, of how the power of our mind can land us in extraordinary circumstances. Each story is true and will inspire you to discover the thread of your own greatest dreams and show you how to live them here and now.

You will laugh, cry and be inspired to discover the greater purpose in your own life.

Third in the Series,

Conscious Women— Conscious Careers

Life Changing Stories of Discovering Diving Vocation, Living on Purpose & Transformational Experiences in Our Careers

In this powerful collection, *women* share stories of encounters with the divine in their careers. Each story shows that by following our intuition, dreams and inner guidance we can live a life filled with meaning, purpose and joy.

This inspiring book contains stories from some of the world's foremost women authorities on health, healing and spirituality, plus stories from ordinary women on their real experiences of finding their true calling, purpose or vocation and how to live their highest dreams.

Whether you're looking for your true calling, or wish to know how to be more fulfilled in the career you've chosen, Conscious Women Conscious Careers can provide hope and answers to some of your deepest questions. Why am I here? Do I have a greater purpose? How do I find meaning here and now with my own unique talents and gifts? Each story brings us closer to the truth of our own divine nature and teaches us that we can live a joyous fulfilling life here and now.

Message from the Publisher

MOTHERS! WONDERFUL, WONDERFUL MOTHERS!

Mother's Day is a splendid tribute, but why don't we celebrate their unselfish legacy all 365 days of the year – like they deserve?

In her transforming way of connecting so splendidly with talented, renowned authors, Darlene Montgomery has again brought out the best of Conscious Women in this book of short stories written from the heart of being a mother. Three prior *Conscious Women* titles, including the most recent *Conscious Women, Conscious Careers* have established Montgomery in the role of leading a tradition within White Knight Books seasonal offerings.

When meditating after reading each story you will feel that you almost know the story that must be behind what you just read. If it seems familiar, look at your own life first.

All are blessed to know that Mothers mean so much to our society.

~ *Bill Belfontaine*
Publisher

Contributors

BARBARA ALLPORT is a therapist in private practice in Toronto and Bancroft Ontario, Canada. She resides in Bancroft with her two cats. She can be reached at barballport@fcicanada.net.

RHOBBIN ALEXIS has her own radio show, *The Mystic with Rhobbin Alexis,* which airs on Talk Radio 1340 KIST-AM in Santa Barbara, California. Rhobbin's first book *Raising Humanity, Birthing Our Global Family* by Rhobbin Alexis and 22 storytellers is available through www.amazon.com and has a very compelling endorsement from Darlene on the back cover! *Raising Humanity* was created to raise consciousness through sharing soulful stories of people who remember that we are the future teachers of peace. She believes it is our ultimate responsibility to future generations. The very soul of humanity is at stake. Rhobbin can be reached at www.mysticradio.us or call her for a private reading at 310-273-8655 ext 3.

KAREN MARIE AREL retired from a successful career as the Executive Director of the Kennebunk Kennebunkport Chamber of Commerce in 2003. Pursuing her love of writing, she has published short stories about her family and herself as well as informative business articles. Her work has appeared in The Portland Press Herald, The Palm Beach Post, The Maine Women's Journal, Chicken Soup for the Recovering Soul, Daily Inspirations and the website www.vickimonroe.com <http://www.vickimonroe.com/>. Her goal is to one day compile her short stories of humor, inspiration and courage into a collection that will help others. Karen lives with her husband Jerry in Kennebunk, Maine. She may be reached at karel@adelphia.net

SYBIL BARBOUR resides in Kitchener, Ontario with her husband and an aged cat. She is a retired registered nurse and midwife. Sybil recently fulfilled a lifelong dream of traveling to Italy, Greece, Scotland, and New Zealand. You can contact her at sybilbarbour@sympatico.ca.

JOAN BORYSENKO, PH.D. has a powerfully clear personal vision: to bring science, medicine, psychology and spirituality together in the service of healing. Her brilliance as a scientist, clinician and teacher have placed her on the leading edge of the mind-body revolution, and she has become a world-renowned spokesperson for this new approach to health, sharing her pioneering work with a gentle graciousness, enthusiasm and humility.

Trained as both a medical scientist and a psychologist, Dr. Borysenko has gone beyond her traditional academic training and developed depth and breadth in a number of fields including behavioral medicine, stress and well-being, psychoneuroimmunology, women's health, creativity and the great spiritual traditions of the world. She completed her doctorate in medical sciences at the Harvard Medical School where she also completed three post-doctoral fellowships in experimental pathology, behavioral medicine and psychoneuroimmunology and where she was instructor in medicine until 1988.

Also a licensed psychologist, Dr. Borysenko was co-founder and former Director of the Mind-Body clinical programs at two Harvard Medical School teaching hospitals, now merged as the Beth Israel/Deaconess Medical Center in Boston. These programs were the foundation for her 1987 classic New York Times bestseller *Minding the Body, Mending the Mind.*

Dr. Borysenko is a spell-binding lecturer and workshop leader who blends science, psychology and spirituality in a unique and powerful way. Her presentations are full of humor and personal anecdotes as well as the latest scientific research and practical exercises for both personal and professional growth. Her eleven books are a complete library of healing, combining scholarly wisdom with the language of the heart, and bringing body and soul together with unprecedented clarity and sophistication.

CYNTHIA BRIAN, NY Times co-author of best selling book, *Chicken Soup for the Gardener's Soul*, author of Be the Star You Are!®, 99 Gifts for Living, Loving, Laughing, and Learning to Make a Difference; The Business of Show Business; Daddy's Hands, Mommy's Heart, Children's Memories; and Miracle Moments®. is an internationally acclaimed key note speaker, parenting expert, personal growth consultant, host of radio and TV shows, syndicated columnist and media, acting, success presentation coach. Cynthia is also the Home, Garden, and Lifestyle Expert at ClubMom.com offering tips for women around the world and enjoys being an editor at Your Life Magazine. When she is not in her garden, Cynthia and her daughter, Heather Brittany, known as The Stelle Donne Goddess Gals, work together in films, television, radio, commercials, print, and numerous speaking/ writing endeavors. Starstyle® Productions, LLC, PO Box 422, Moraga, Ca. 94556. Email: cynthia@star-style.com, www.star-style.com and www.goddessgals.com.

VICKI BRUCE has been in libraries since her two amazing children were just babies. She started her career as a volunteer librarian in a small library in Richmond, Ontario. Through a transfer in her husband's career she found herself in a very spiritual area of Ontario. She now calls Sunderland home. Vicki will be releasing a preteen novel "Spaced Out" in September 2006. If you want to learn more about Vicki, her website is www.vickilionart.com

MARLENE CHAPELLE is a talented teacher, costumer, chef and carpenter. As a member of the ECKANKAR Clergy she performs weddings and other sacerdotal functions. She has appeared on television to share stories of her spiritual adventures.

BRENDA CHISHOLM lives in Burlington, Ontario, Canada with her husband, Robin, and two daughters, Kendra and Marina Grace. She works full-time in a software company; writes in the evenings for an on-line community magazine; has a weird record collection of 45 rpms from the 70s and 80s, and, enjoys singing. You can reach Brenda at (905) 639-4568.

DEBORAH DAVIS is an active member of the Ottawa Police Service. She is an accomplished singer and is a member of the Ottawa Police Choir and the Temple of ECK Choir. She is a Reiki Master and continues to study energy medicine and alternative healing. She hopes to start a second career in Transformational Healing.

NANCY LEE DOIGE lives in Aurora, Ontario, Canada, where she developed a national education program on transplantation and organ donation for grade five through eight students. The Classroom Connections "Gift of Life" Education Program is currently in 7,500 schools across Canada. Nancy draws on her education in family studies at Ryerson University, her work with children in elementary schools and her deeply moving experience when her son Ryan died. Visit her at www.classroom-connections.com or www.ryanshope.com.

MAGIE DOMINIC was born in Corner Brook Newfoundland. She studied at The Art Institute of Pittsburgh; New School University; and Franklin Furnace. Her memoir, *The Queen of Peace Room*, Wilfrid Laurier University Press was nominated for Book of the Year,

ForeWord Magazine – 2003, for The Judy Grahn Award – 2003 and nominated for CWSA/ACEF Book Award – 2004. Her writing and artwork have been published, printed, exhibited or produced in over one hundred quarterlies, newspapers, magazines, anthologies, theatre productions, librettos, art galleries and books. One of the founding members of the Off-Off Broadway movement of the sixties and a member of Poets Fast for Peace during the Vietnam War, she has walked with Ginsberg, given poetry readings with Moondog, written poetry, short stories, essays, and non-fiction, and developed a creative writing curriculum for high school students at risk. Her art work includes installation, collage, illustration and photography and has been exhibited in Toronto and New York, including a presentation at the United Nations.

DALIA GESSER attended Purchase University, one of the State Universities of New York, majoring in dance. Veering towards theatre, she then studied theatre arts at the Canadian Mime School moving on to perform with the Canadian Mime Theatre for their last season. After creating her original one woman children's shows which combined drama, mime, mask and circus skills under the name Compact Theatre, she performed for over twenty years touring throughout Ontario. Since 1998 she has been sharing her theatre arts skills with students of all ages in the Kingston Region. She lives with her husband, two sons, dog and ferrets in Battersea, just north of Kingston in beautiful lake country.

SHEILA GOOD (nee Barbour) wrote this poem as a young adult with a heartache for the whereabouts of her step-sister Georgie, whom she had not seen since she was a child. Georgie and Sheila were finally reunited in 1997, knitting together the hearts of the two women and their families. Sheila says, "Being reunited with Georgie has made such a difference in my life. The term 'step-sister' does not do justice to the unconditional love that she shows toward me and my family." Sheila lives with her husband Stephen in Lubbock, Texas, where they home school their five children.

ELLIE BRAUN-HALEY lives in an old country home, where she can walk the countryside and feel the nearness of God. She says "There will be more stories because I believe the contacts will continue, even increase. The tie to my son remains and I hold on to the words he gave me in a dream. "But mom, death is not forever." The book, *A Little Door, A Little Light*, ISBN 1-894446-92-X is available through Eagle Valley Research (evrcanada.com) Look on Menu for Eagle Creek Publishers the web address) or by contacting Ellie (shaley@telusplanet.net)

MONIQUE HOWAT is a self-esteem youth motivator and the founder of Confident Girls and Guys. She presents lively workshops at elementary and high schools in and around the Toronto area. Monique is an energetic public speaker and offers comprehensive "Train your Trainers" sessions twice yearly. You can visit her website at www.confidentgirlsguys.com.

SANDRA IRVINE is currently living in Barrie, Ontario, working as a registered nurse in the community. Her work involves caring for many palliative patients and she is interested in branching out into alternative therapies. She is physically active, involved in many sports and activities including yoga. Her interests include studying Reflexology and she is currently working on obtaining her Level 2 Reiki certification. She has an avid interest in studying dreams, angels, spirituality and past lives. To contact Sandra send email to butterfly961@msn.com.

JOANNA KOKALOVSKI was born in Elblag, in the southern part of Poland. As a young child she enjoyed art and writing classes. She had a childhood filled with fun and lots of imaginary adventures. But the real adventure started when her family immigrated to Toronto, Canada in 1980. There she immersed herself in learning English and French, assimilating to the new and exciting culture. After attending high school, Joanna studied at University of Toronto. She attained two degrees: Specialist in Research in Psychology and major in Biology. Currently, she is working in medical research at the University Health Network (Toronto Hospital). In August 2005 she married Alen, her sweetheart of 10 years in a lovely Polish/Macedonian wedding. Joanna loves to read inspirational books, paint and converse in French. She is looking forward to being a mother someday and hopes to be a great mother as her mother was to her.

JACQUELINE KRAMER has been practicing and studying Buddhism for 27 years. She began sticking her toes into Eastern philosophy when she was 16 years old by pouring over a copy of Zen Flesh, Zen Bones and practicing transcendental meditation. She was attracted to the practicality and beauty of the teachings. Her study and practice began in earnest when she met her meditation teacher Annagarika Dhamma Dinna in 1976.

By the time Jacqueline had become pregnant with her daughter Nicole, she had been practicing Buddhism for three years. Jacqueline had been taught to apply the Buddha's teachings to everyday life so it was natural for her to apply the teachings to her pregnancy, birth, mothering and homemaking.

Aware of the dangers of nuclear arms proliferation, threats to the environment, and tender from her birthing experience, Jacqueline devoted herself to being a part of the solution. Not long after making this commitment, Jacqueline began writing Buddha Mom. "I wrote the book I wanted to read, but couldn't find, when I was a young mother," Jacqueline says. "I had read that being a homemaker was a distraction on the path to spiritual development, but my experience was just the opposite. This is why I wrote Buddha Mom, to share that support and insight with others." Jacqueline's practice is applying mindfulness and compassion to everyday activities.

Nicole is now in her 20s. Jacqueline is currently living in rural Sonoma County, California. She is the director of a spiritual growth study group and provides spiritual counseling as a Religious Science Practitioner. Jacqueline holds a Bachelor of Arts degree in painting and sculpture from Bennington College. She teaches art and music appreciation to seniors. Jacqueline sings with a swing big band and performs one-woman shows. She is a freelance writer. For more on Jacqueline visit: http://www.whatanicewebsite.com/buddhamom/index.htm.

SUZANNE THOMAS LAWLOR is the Director of Education and Public Relations for Humanity in Unity, a nonprofit organization dedicated to bringing relief and upliftment to all races, cultures and religions. Suzanne lives in the San Francisco Bay area and continues her work as a freelance writer. For the last 30 years she has taught meditation and studied the development of consciousness through Vedic and Eastern traditions. Along the way her life has been graced by many travels and many teachers, including Maharishi Mahesh Yogi and a handful of extraordinary Divine Mothers who reflect the Truth that: God is both Father and Mother. She is currently working on a book on the Kathars, the mystical branch of Christianity founded by Mary Magdalene. Suzanne can be contacted at riverofgrace@aol.com.

JACQUELYN MANTELL has always maintained an avid interest in healing ever since being wrongly diagnosed as an epileptic when she was a teenager. She has traveled the world over with her doctor-husband to attend medical seminars about holistic medicine and new methods of treatment. They work side by side in their medical clinic where Jacquelyn, among other duties, facilitates patient healing by doing holistic counseling. This includes nutritional education along with emotional, mental and spiritual guidance. As co-hosts of a medical talk show, she and her husband discussed all aspects of holistic healing. Jacquelyn loves to write and teach others about spiritual awareness and how to recognize God's love in their daily lives. She has been a member of the Eckankar clergy for many years. Contact Jackie at bluestar9@adelphia.net.

JANET MATTHEWS is a writer, editor, speaker, teacher and co-author of the Canadian Bestseller, *Chicken Soup for the Canadian Soul.* Janet has been a guest on countless television and radio talk shows across Canada, and is a key-note speaker for major organization across North America. Janet is also working with Daniel Keenan to produce a book-sized version of "*The Navy's Baby,*" a wonderfully inspiring story that appears in *Chicken Soup for the Parent's Soul.* You can contact Janet at: Chicken Soup for the Canadian Soul, 2- 9225 Leslie Street, Richmond Hill Ontario, L4B 3H6.

SABRINA MOHAMEDALI completed her Early Childhood Education degree in 1999 and progressed with Early Intervention and Resource Teaching. She has worked throughout centres in Ontario and Alberta and founded Sabrina's Kid's Cove in Edmonton. Currently she is studying at Etrat University and lives in Ontario with her husband and two beautiful children. She has traveled to the Middle East and Africa as well as throughout Canada and Europe.

She is constantly researching ways to better the childhood experience and give parents the tools to raise a conscious society.

CAROL MATTHEWS-O'CONNOR is a daughter/mother/wife /friend/cook/animal lover/children's book author/and second-grade teacher in a migrant farm worker town in South Florida where she enjoys grand adventures with her students. She has published two beginning reader picture books. Children's literature tops the list of her favorite things, along with riding horses, hiking mountain trails (especially in the West), music, and cooking for friends.

DEBBIE MCMECHAN describes herself as a child of the southwest Manitoba prairies. Together with her husband, Tony, and three children, Danielle, Justin and Paige, she makes her living off the land, raising cattle and growing crops.

MARILYN J. MILNE was born and raised on the raincoast of Vancouver, British Columbia, Canada. She has produced and directed music concerts and stage productions, has written several feature film screenplays, and completed a socio-ecological New Age novel entitled, *Universal Tides: Barbed Wire Blues.* Milne's articles have been published in magazines in the USA and Canada. Her interests are writing, art, spirituality, environmentalism, travel and people. For more information go to her website: www.UniversalTides.com; or write her at: info@universaltides.com

BONITA "BONNIE" O'NEILL is a retired school teacher. She is the adoptive mother of one son. She is widowed and lives in Fenelon Falls, Ontario, Canada with three very spoiled cats. Spare time is spent curling, running, volunteering and writing.

PATRICIA ORWIN resides in Comox, BC. where she works in the health food industry assisting others in taking charge of their health on all levels. She has always felt a deep connection to nature, which inspires her love of writing inspirational poetry. You can contact Patricia at patriciaorwin@yahoo.ca.

JUDY PRANG is proud to have served as editor for this book. She resides in Kingston, Ontario, Canada with her husband, Cal. A Senior Manager for a major financial institution, she volunteers her time on the Board of Directors of The Elizabeth Fry Society of Kingston, an organization that supports women in conflict, or in danger of coming into conflict with the law. During the last 10 years while gaining experience in communication, group facilitation, motivation and organizational effectiveness, Judy learned that story telling is the best way to celebrate our spiritual journey. Judy is a contributing author to *Conscious Women, Conscious Lives, Book 2* and *Conscious Women, Conscious Careers*. A mother of two grown daughters and grandmother of five, she continues to write inspirational stories from her own life experiences and is exploring ways to help others share their own. Judy is currently working on her first book and can be reached at judyprang@hotmail.com.

BETTY JANE RAPIN, nicknamed BJ, is a clergywoman who is currently the Eckankar Spiritual Services Director for the state of Pennsylvania. She is a contributing author to *Rhyme 'n Rhythm*, a book of poetry. Her works have been published on the web and in newsletters, magazines and newspapers. She had a bi-weekly column in her neighborhood newspaper and is currently working on her first book. Betty has been a guest on several television and radio shows to speak about a variety of spiritual subjects. Now retired after thirty six years in the restaurant business, she continues to freelance her writing, teach adult education classes and speak publicly. Her web page, *Stories From The Heart* address is www.bj.zelf.us. She can also be reached at bea.jayhusing@aol.com

LAURA REAVE, PH. D. has been a writer, editor, and English professor for fifteen years. Her current research interest is spiritual leadership, and she has an article forthcoming on this topic in the journal, *Leadership Quarterly*. She also has particular interest in spiritual poetry. She is proud to serve as the editor for *Conscious Women, Conscious Lives Two* and *Conscious Women Conscious Careers*. She can be reached at lreave@ody.ca.

SHEILA KINDELLAN-SHEEHAN is a native of Québec. She holds an MA in English from Concordia University. Her work has been published in *Room of One's Own, The Globe and Mail,* read on *CBC's First Person Singular, Radio One, CBC Montreal, and CJAD. Sheila's Take,* her first collection of short stories, a Shoreline publication in 2003, has twice been cited on the bestseller list. Ms Kindellan is also a popular speaker on the Québec circuit.

VERONICA A. SHOFFSTALL was born September 24, 1952 in New York City, where she currently lives and works. She is a member of the Bahá'í Faith, which teaches that there is one God, one religion, and one human race and our challenge for the age is to act on that reality, appreciate our diversity and live and work in unity.

CATHERINE STAFFORD, M.ED., is a therapist and writer. Her essays and articles have appeared in several publications, including the *Globe and Mail* and the *Montreal Gazette* newspapers. She is currently working on a book of non-fiction chronicling her experiences in coping with recurrent miscarriages and two life-threatening pregnancies.

Catherine grew up in Montreal and obtained her Master of Education in Counseling Psychology degree from McGill University, as well as national certification through the Canadian Counseling Association. She has worked in universities, non-profit organizations, and in private counseling practice settings. Her areas of special interest include cross-cultural counseling, coping with chronic health issues, women's issues, and exploring the mind-body connection. She may be reached at *cathstaff@yahoo.com*.

JENNIFER GAY SUMMERS' *work has appeared in Chicken* Soup for the Dog Lover's Soul (2005), *Chicken Soup for the Cat Lover's Soul* (2005), *Adoptive Families Magazine*, *Orange County Family Magazine*, *Inland Empire Family Magazine*, and *Whole Life Times*.

CHRISTINE SWITZER was a photographer at the time of her daughter's struggle with Anorexia. Her work was featured on The Life Network. Today, Chris is studying to become a veterinary assistant. To contact Christine Switzer email: cswitzer@rogers.com.

SHARI TALLON is an International Recording Artist, Composer, Musician and Educator. She has produced over 15 projects for children and resources for educators. She also works with children with special needs using music as a therapy. You can visit her web site at www.shariandjerry.com

JEAN VERSTEEG'S studies in Fine Arts and Social Work have led her into a varied and stimulating career, from teaching design and color in New Zealand and Australia to producing films and videos in Australia and Canada. Currently Jean exhibits her paintings, writes poetry and works in her garden. She is also working on a documentary on Canadian artist, Norval Morrisseau.

DARYL WOOD has expressed herself creatively almost since birth through music, art and words. She has been published in *The Toronto Star* and periodicals throughout North America. Founder of the *Spirited Woman Magazine* and Healing Rock Retreat on the shores of Lake Huron in Tobermory, Ontario, Daryl cherishes her life journey while helping others stay connected to their spirit. Her address is 417 Eagle Road, Tobermory, Ontario, Canada, N0H 2R0 and her web site is www.darylwood.com.

MARION WOODMAN is a writer, international teacher and workshop leader, and Jungian analyst. With over a half-million copies in print, she is one of the most widely read authors on analytical and feminine psychology of our times. Marion Woodman is a graduate of the C.G. Jung Institute in Zurich. Her best selling book *Addiction to Perfection* is considered to be a landmark study on the spiritual and psychological roots of addiction in women. Other books include *The Ravaged Bridegroom; Leaving My Father's House; The Maiden King;* and *The Pregnant Virgin.* Her newest book, *Bone: Dying into Life* (Viking Press, September 2000) is the story of her dealing with and healing from uterine cancer and transforming her life in the process. For more about Marion visit www.mwoodmanfoundation.org.

COLLEEN YEATES is Judy Prang's daughter and one of the proofreaders of this book. A busy single Mom of two boys, she also lives in Kingston, Ontario. Colleen has returned to school to become a nurse and can be reached at c.yeates@sympatico.ca.

Permissions / Notes

An Everlasting Farewell, reprinted by permission of Marion Woodman
   © 2003 Marion Woodman
Honoring My Dreams, reprinted by permission of Brenda Chisholm
   © 2000 Brenda Chisholm
It's A Piece of Cake, reprinted by permission of Janet Matthews
   © 2000 Janet Matthews
My Mother – A Mystery, reprinted by permission of Sheila Kindellan-Sheehan
   © 2001 Sheila Kindellan-Sheehan
My Mother's Last Gift, reprinted by permission of Joan Borysenko
   © 2003 Joan Borysenko
To See My Skye Again, reprinted by permission of Patricia Orwin
   © 2001 Patricia Orwin
A Love Everlasting, reprinted by permission of Suzanne Thomas Lawlor
   © 1996 Suzanne Thomas Lawlor
The Hug, reprinted by permission of Barbara Allport © 2005 Barbara Allport
A Gift of Love, reprinted by permission of Sybil Barbour © 2005 Sybil Barbour
From Spark to Flame, reprinted by permission of Monique Howat
   © 2005 Monique Howat
Mother and Daughter Reunion, reprinted by permission of Betty Jane Rapin
   © 2006 Betty Jane Rapin
Coming Home to Oz, reprinted by permission of Christine Switzer
   © 2006 Christine Switzer
My Mother: My Spiritual Teacher, reprinted by permission of Jacqueline Kramer
   © 2006 Jacqueline Kramer
Like Mother, Like Father, reprinted by permission of Rhobbin Alexis
   © 2006 Rhobbin Alexis
A Soul Decision, reprinted by permission of Marlene Chapelle
   © 2006 Marlene Chapelle
You Learn, reprinted by permission of Veronica A. Shoffstall
   © 1971 Veronica A. Shoffstall
A Knowing, reprinted by permission of Jennifer Gay Summers
   © 2006 Jennifer Gay
Miracle Mom, reprinted by permission of Vicki Bruce © 2006 Vicki Bruce
My Mother's Old Soul, reprinted by permission of Joanna Kokalovski
   © 2006 Joanna Kokalovski
Smart Food, reprinted by permission of Shari Tallon © 2006 Shari Tallon

OTHER WHITE KNIGHT BOOKS

Visit our website
www.whiteknightbooks.ca
or request catalogue.